ENCOUNTERSWITHGOD²
True Stories of Teens with a Sacred Calling

© 2006 Standard Publishing, Cincinnati, Ohio.
A division of Standex International Corporation.
All rights reserved. No part of this book may be reproduced in any form, except for brief quotations in reviews, without the written permission of the publisher.

refuge™ is a trademark of Standard Publishing.

Printed in the United States of America.

Project editor: Robert Irvin
Cover and interior design: Scott Ryan

All Scripture quotations, unless otherwise indicated, are taken from the HOLY BIBLE, NEW INTERNATIONAL VERSION®. NIV®. Copyright © 1973, 1978, 1984 by International Bible Society. Used by permission of Zondervan Publishing House. All rights reserved.

Scriptures marked *NLT* are taken from the Holy Bible, New Living Translation, copyright © 1996. Used by permission of Tyndale House Publishers, Inc., Wheaton, Ill. 60189. All rights reserved.

Anbesol® is a registered trademark of Wyeth Consumer Healthcare, which is not affiliated with Standard Publishing.
Jell-O® is a registered trademark of Kraft Foods, Inc., which is not affiliated with Standard Publishing.

ISBN 0-7847-1867-9

Library of Congress Cataloging-in-Publication Data:
   Encounters with God : true stories of teens on a sacred journey / compiled by Kelly Carr.
      p. cm.
Includes bibliographical references and index.
   ISBN 0-7847-1767-2 (pbk.)
1. Christian teenagers—Religious life. I. Carr, Kelly, 1977–
BV4531.3.E53 2005
248.8'3—dc22   2005006031

13 12 11 10 09 08 07 06   7 6 5 4 3 2 1

ENCOUNTERS WITH GOD²

True Stories of Teens with a Sacred Calling

Compiled by Kelly Carr

refuge
an imprint of
Standard Publishing
www.rfgbooks.com

To My precious Kaelyn. I hope that some day, when you're old enough to read, this book will encourage you to seek your own calling from God.

CONTENTS

Introduction 9

GOD, IS THAT YOU?
Seeing God's True Grace 14
We Don't Need Another Hero 19
Bad Hair Day 24
Breaking Free 27
End of Search 32
My Fairy Tale 34
Beating Addictions, Finding God 38
"I Need Some Help Here!" 44
Real Fear 47
The Nightmare Before My Baptism 51
Away From the Window 53
Facing My Fears 58
Fulfilled 62
Wonderful Counselor 63

LOOK WHAT I CAN DO!
I Felt Like a Loser 68
Headaches, Bug Bites, and Hunger 72
Looking At Life through Death 75
I Love You 79
Step Out and Be Seen 80
Rock On! 84
Storms Rage, God Conquers 88
Never Really Alone 94
The Music on My Heart 96
Unique Individuals 101
The Band Camp Dare 103
Happy Friday 108
A Coffeehouse Witness 109

Sitting in Silence 113
Remembering My Grandfather 117

WHAT'S THE **POINT?**

Fighting for Hope 122
Never Alone 127
No Valley Low Enough 128
At the Point of Pain 131
Best of Times, Worst of Times 135
Solid Rock 139
My World of Tears 144
God's Big Dreams 145
Discovering I Was Bipolar 150
I Was So Hurt! 155
The Pain and Gain of Suffering 159
Into the Light 164
Unanswered Prayer 165

CAN I GET **A DO-OVER?**

Busted! 170
Daddy's Not-So-Little Girl 175
Beyond All Barriers 179
There Was a Time 183
God Uses Even Me 184
I Lost My Cool 188
Thank You 192
Unconscious 194
Scared of the Dark 197
When Friends Fight 201
"It Will Be OK" 206
You Found Me 210
A Living Hope 211
A Life-Changing Experience 214
T-shirt Testimony 217

I'LL SHOW YOU HOW

Looking for God 222
The Power of a Mentor 225
Never Know 229
Nothing to Fear 230
An Unlikely Friendship 235
The Touch 237
Daily Warrior 239
Audience of One 244
Waiting for Harvest 246
Getting Your Hands Dirty 250
Being Friends with a Wiccan 255
The Adventure 260
Final Thoughts 265

MUSIC ARTISTS

Bethany Dillon 266
Casting Crowns 268
Jeremy Camp 270
LA Symphony 272
Mat Kearney 274
Nicole C. Mullen 276
Seventh Day Slumber 278
ZOEgirl 280

TOPICAL INDEX 282

INTRODUCTION

The question hung in the air before me. How I answered would define my future.

I was in my high school Sunday school class and the teacher was talking about our relationships with God. He said it didn't matter if we had grown up in church or if our parents had a relationship with God—deciding to follow Jesus was a personal decision that each of us had to make. I talked with the teacher afterward, and I still recall the question he asked me point-blank: "Have you made your faith your own?"

I just stood there. No one had ever asked me that before. Had I been going through the motions of being raised in church without putting meaning to my actions? If so, I needed to decide if Jesus was for real and take a look at how he fit into my life. Or had I already committed my life to God and become his follower? If so, I needed to take the next step by fully submitting to his Holy Spirit and listening to his guidance on a daily basis.

I thought about that question for a while. (Obviously, it has stayed in my mind years later.) At that point in my life, I decided that, yes, my faith truly had become my own. I had decided to make my faith in Jesus the central point of my life. I was raised to know *about* God, but I also had said that I wanted a relationship *with* God through his son Jesus.

So the next thing I needed to do was to begin pursuing God's calling for my life.

God's Calling

What's a "calling" anyway? It sounds like something preachers and missionaries and really spiritual people talk about. Actually, God calls everyone, whether you feel spiritual or not. And he has a different plan for each person's life.

God's calling, essentially, means the things God has designed for you to do for his kingdom. God uses a combination of the abilities and passions he put inside you, plus your life experiences and opportunities. All add up to *you* doing something for *his* glory.

Figuring out God's calling for you probably won't happen overnight. In fact, God will have different callings for you at different stages of your life. You can spend the rest of your days keeping your eyes and ears open for his leading.

So why not get started now?

This Book

Encounters with God 2 is filled with stories of people who are somewhere in the process of figuring out God's calling for their lives.

- In *section one* you'll read about people who took their first steps into a relationship with God and had to figure out who he was and if he was worth following.
- In *section two* authors share their newfound confidence as they've begun to recognize the wonderful qualities God placed inside them.
- *Section three* relates the stories of people's difficult experiences that made them question whether God was really present in their lives.
- In *section four* others discovered the comfort of a second chance after they had turned away from God's calling to follow their own desires.
- And finally, in *section five*, authors describe their excitement as they began to reach out and help others discover God's calling for their lives.

At the end of this book are more fun stories about the music artists who appear in *Encounters with God 2* and an index to search the book's stories by topic. There you'll also find additional Scriptures you can read for further biblical perspective on those topics.

Somewhere in all these stories, you'll read things that remind you of your own situation. And I hope that, along the way, you begin to discover God's calling for your life.

—KLC

GOD, IS THAT YOU?

"The LORD came and stood there, calling as at the other times..."

—1 Samuel 3:10

SEEING GOD'S TRUE GRACE

As I began to reflect on my life, I realized things I needed to change.

As I sat at my grandmother's memorial service, I couldn't help but reflect on how short life is. It says in Ecclesiastes that it's so much better to go to a funeral than to go to a party (Ecclesiastes 7:2). Funerals do force us to think about how precious life is.

A Life Passed

I sat there with my cousins and other family members. My grandmother had eight children, twenty-nine grandkids, and fourteen great-grandkids. It was a powerful moment for all of us because it became clear how God had blessed all of us through this one woman.

My grandmother was born an orphan and grew up to be a mighty woman of God. She never did great things. She was a pastor's wife most of her life, until Grandpa passed away. She did just the smallest things, but at the same time I realized we're all blessed by her life, by this small little woman who would have admitted that she didn't have it all figured out. The moment made me realize just how much I want to be like my grandmother—to one day have grandchildren who are blessed by me and have God somehow, through my life, inspire them.

As I began to reflect on my life and what it would take to emulate my grandmother, I realized things I needed to change. There are so many things that God is trying to teach me. God has been making it really clear how I'm wrapped up in myself.

A Realization Gained

Growing up in church, I know a lot of the answers and have a lot of head knowledge, so a lot of times I can coast through hard times or struggles. I can counsel myself without ever looking weak to others. I get myself to the point where I say, *Well, I don't really struggle with that.* I pretend I'm strong.

But I think God is bringing my faults to the surface in order to give me humility. He's showed me how I love to talk about people and how I love to talk about myself. Both grow into the ugliest things, things like jealousy and gossip and being judgmental. I realize I'm not as strong as I think I am.

> **I often see God as being very full of wrath. But God is also full of grace and compassion.**

Even though those realizations can be overwhelming, I'm diving into how faithful God is even in the middle of it. I just feel like God is so understanding of our weaknesses. I've been very humbled and embarrassed, in a way, about my thoughts and how I act toward people and the motivations behind those actions. But at the same time, I know God is going to stand by me. Hopefully, at the end of it, I will have a heart that is more like his. I know that I'll always struggle, but I hope that somehow I can fall out of the mold and distance myself from my struggles. That's where I'm at right now.

A Grace Found

I've learned a lot about God's grace from a film called *Luther*. It's an incredible film about the life of Martin Luther (the Catholic monk who began a movement that resulted in most Protestant churches today). There are so many things in that movie that just stick with me. It moves me every time I watch it. In the movie, Luther wrestles with the concept of God being as emotionless and rigid as the Catholic Church of the sixteenth century saw him.

As soon as Luther figured out who Jesus was through reading the Gospels, everything changed. There's one scene in the movie where Luther is in a church cemetery burying this little boy who committed suicide. It was illegal back then because the church taught that suicides automatically went to hell. The parents are standing around and, little by little, the town is gathering around. All Luther said to them was, "God must be mercy."

That just stuck with me because I often see God as being very full of wrath. But God is also full of grace and compassion. That's what the song "Be Near Me" (on my album *Imagination*) is about—my struggle in seeing God like that because I know what I deserve. And I know that God doesn't give me what I deserve.

A Door Opened

The passage that always comes to my mind is when Jesus said, "To whom much is given much is required" (Luke 12:48). I just wish people knew what a mess I am and how much we all are in the same boat. We're all struggling with the same things and needing grace daily.

> *We're all struggling with the same things and needing grace daily.*

People think because I'm in the spotlight that my life is problem-free. Of course, it isn't. It's a funny thing. I think there are people who just pull it off better, and then there are people like me. I feel like as soon as I meet people, they're not star-struck any more. People forget that they want my autograph because they see that I really am a mess.

It's truly an honor to have that door open to share with others that I struggle and to share how faithful and how sweet God has been. I enjoy it. I don't deserve the privilege in any way, but it's really fun to see God move through that.

So every day I'm trying to be a person whose life will bless others. I'm trying to be like Grandma. And with God's help and his grace, maybe I'll get there one day. Sure, I'll have struggles. I'll backslide and fall into old habits. But God's grace is sufficient for me. I know with him by my side, there's nothing we can't handle together.

by Brian Coates

WE DON'T NEED ANOTHER HERO

I was so captivated that I even believed I was Superman.

When I was ten I was obsessed with Superman. The Man of Steel was my hero. I could not get enough of him. I would spend hours in front of my parents' television watching the movies. And when the movies weren't on, it would be *Superfriends*. Well, *Superfriends* or *Scooby Doo*. (If only Superman had been given a cameo role on the latter, instead of Batman & Robin or the Harlem Globetrotters, my childhood might have been happier.) But, I digress . . . back to Superman.

Super Dreams

Not only did I have the action figure that made a punching motion when you squeezed his knees together, but I had the Superman underwear to match! I was so captivated I even believed I *was* Superman.

On summer afternoons I would tie on my very own cape and fly, soaring high over the Metropolis skyline.

I can only imagine how ridiculous this looked to my neighbors. Mainly because I wasn't really flying. I was running around my backyard with my arms stuck out straight ahead of me. (If you've ever done this, you know that running with your arms in this position makes it difficult to maintain your balance.)

And not only was I not even flying, my cape wasn't even a cape. Instead, it was a beach towel with the logo of the insurance company my mom worked for. And it was pinned around my neck using a safety pin that at one time held my diapers around my waist. You know the kind, about two inches long with a plastic yellow duck as the latch. And I wasn't afraid to wear the duck pin either. Why? Because I was Superman. When you're Superman, you can pretty much wear whatever you want and not have to worry about anyone talking trash.

All Grown Up?

That was a number of years ago, though. Since then, I have grown up. I have graduated from college and been working for a few years. I have matured. If you were to ask me today whether I still thought I could be Superman, my answer would be much more sensible and levelheaded. The answer would be "No, of course not." And I think you know where I am going here, because the answer is pretty obvious: Instead, I would be Spider-Man.

When I was ten, I needed a reality check. The whole history of Superman is a stretch. An alien who is sent to earth and, under the effect of the sun, has superhuman powers? That is about as far-fetched as thinking a man could survive underwater and communicate with sea creatures!

Spider-Man, however, is an entirely different story. Spider-Man was just a normal guy—a normal guy who accidentally got bit by a genetically engineered super-spider. Not only is it plausible, but completely possible! It could happen to anyone. It could happen to me! All I need is to be in the right place, at the right time, with the right escaped super-spider, and BAM! . . . I'm Spider-Man.

Pieces of Ourselves

Really, though, I think the reason I have wanted to be a superhero from such a young age is the same reason every person has wanted to be one: Superheroes best embody our greatest qualities. They are strong. They are fearless. They are selfless. They are compassionate. They are caring. They are loving. They are human. They hurt for the people they love, and they long for their love to be returned.

Superheroes best embody our greatest qualities.

We identify with them. We want to be them. We sit in theaters watching the visual narratives of their stories unfold, and we see in them pieces of ourselves. In our minds we project our own image on the big screen, stopping the subway train just before it plunges into the river, saving the day. We watch the credits roll, wishing the world really did have a hero like the one in the movie we just watched.

What we do not always realize is that the world did have a superhero, and he first stepped onto the soil a couple thousand years ago. But instead of a fictional hero sent from a far off planet to a Kansas farm, or one created by a freak insect bite in New York City, our hero was sent from heaven to a manger in Bethlehem. He came to earth for no other reason than to save everyone from an evil more dark than any comic book villain ever imagined. That man was Jesus Christ.

> *Jesus wasn't your typical superhero. He had no logo on his chest or spotlight beacon in the sky.*

Truly Heroic

But Jesus wasn't your typical superhero. He wore no cape or costume. He had no logo on his chest or spotlight beacon in the sky. He didn't have a wise cracking sidekick with a catchy tagline. And he didn't try to hide his identity to protect himself or his family. He boldly proclaimed who he was, fearless of the danger it would later bring upon himself and his friends.

Jesus didn't come to earth and not know why he was here. He didn't just find out what God intended of him once he got here. He left heaven knowing full well what he had to do. He knew everything that would happen to him—and he still came. You see, instead of possessing superhero attributes, he was the very definition of those attributes: He was strength. He was fearlessness. He was selflessness. He was compassion. He was love. Everything he did and everything he said defined those attributes.

So the next time you head to the theaters to catch the latest summer blockbuster starring a web-slinging, faster-than-a-speeding-bullet caped crusader, remember this: The world doesn't have a flashy superhero—it has you and me. We may be the closest thing to Jesus some people ever experience.

And so we are called to be strong and fearless and

selfless and compassionate and loving. We are called to stand up for what is right, fight for the weak, show mercy to the poor, and help the sick. We are called to be the heroes.

Are you up to it? I sure hope I am.

by Rebekah Bailey

BAD HAIR DAY

My self-pitying thoughts were suddenly interrupted by the woeful intercom.

Have you ever woken up, looked in the mirror, and no matter how hard you tried, had a thought that, for you, the day would hold not one friendly comment? Well, I had a morning and a mirror and a thought . . . a great big ugly thought just like that, and the world seemed to come down hard on me because of it! Here is my story.

Everyone Will See Me!

It was the day we got back from Christmas break, Tuesday, January 4, 2005. The time was 8:05 AM, and the school tardy bell had just rung. I slipped on the hood of my jacket (hiding my bad hair that plagued my mind), slinked quietly into the classroom, and slipped into my desk, hoping no one would see me.

"It's time for the morning announcements," said Mr. Osborne over the intercom. "If everyone will please take a seat and pay attention."

Well, I was paying attention all right, but not to the announcements. No one else was either. How could they when such an upsetting sight was in their midst? My self-pitying thoughts were suddenly interrupted by the dreadful intercom. Why couldn't it tell us something important, like the school was on fire and we all needed to evacuate immediately?! That way I could go home and bury my head under a pillow! Why?

"We will be meeting in the sanctuary at 9 AM for a school assembly. I apologize for the inconvenience, teachers, but this is very important."

That was it! Could it have gotten any worse? *Everyone in the whole school will see me in this condition,* I thought to myself.

Then after the rest of the announcements, Scripture reading, and prayer, it was time to line up and head for the sanctuary.

A Change in Perspective

Every step felt like a mile. My shoulders were slumped, my head low. I was taking that long, long walk. I had one of those feelings you get when you're walking home to tell your mom you made an F on a test or you're walking into the house to tell your dad you ran over the garden hose with the lawnmower—one of those awful walks.

It was very quiet when we got in the sanctuary. You could hear a needle drop. Mr. Osborne seemed very anxious. Once everyone was seated, he began to speak.

"As most of you know, on December 26, 2004, a very devastating tsunami hit parts of Asia, killing thousands. As a Christian school, we have an opportunity to help."

As he was speaking, I thought to myself, *Thousands have been killed, and I knew about it, and here I am thinking the world has fallen apart because of my bad hair day. I wonder if anyone even notices my hair. Even if they did, would it matter? I can't believe I let this bother me so much that I didn't even care about the loss of thousands of lives.*

Presentable to God

So I said a prayer, asking God forgive me. Then I did the boldest thing I had done all day—I took off my hood. I realized my worried thoughts were just that—thoughts. I began to think of mothers who would do anything to touch their lost child's hair just one more time.

I can't believe I didn't even care about the loss of thousands of lives.

It took the loss of life for me to see what is really important in my own life. My hair crowns my body, which houses my soul. My soul is the only part of me that will last forever, and I'm going to pay more attention to making sure it is fixed up every morning—presentable, not to my friends, but to God.

"The lofty looks of man shall be humbled, and the haughtiness of men shall be bowed down; and the Lord alone shall be exalted in that day" (Isaiah 2:11, *King James Version*).

by Kelli

BREAKING FREE

I felt powerless—I didn't know how to get out.

It seemed like I had everything. As a college sophomore, I was a starter on the women's basketball team at my Division I university. This was after I had an outstanding high school basketball career; my team had won the state championship, and I had been honored as the top player in the state. I went to college on a full basketball scholarship.

That wasn't all. I'd graduated first in my high school class and was continuing to excel at my college studies, where I was majoring in math.

But deep inside, I had emotional needs that weren't being met. I felt I needed to be this perfect person. I was convinced I was flawed on the inside. And I longed to have a relationship in which I could be totally genuine. I wanted someone to know the real me.

Insecurity

An opportunity for friendship came when I met a fellow athlete at college. We became best friends. I felt so comfortable with Erica. There was no pressure to be someone I wasn't, and soon we were together all the time.

Then the unexpected happened. The relationship became physical, something I had never experienced before.

I felt my needs for acceptance and security were being met by Erica, but I was haunted by guilt from which I couldn't escape. It was an inner war—I didn't really want to be there, but yet I did.

The relationship—including the sexual part—continued for the next year or so. Then Erica became interested in another girl. The breakup devastated me. I felt like garbage.

The relationship became physical, something I had never experienced before.

Later, I became friends with Megan, who shared my Christian faith. We also became close. But again, too close. The relationship moved where it shouldn't have gone.

We both realized it was wrong, and we tried to end it, but couldn't. I felt powerless—I didn't know how to get out. I prayed about it, asking God to change me, but it didn't seem to help.

Brokenness

College graduation finally separated Megan and I, as I ended up in Belgium, playing on a women's professional basketball team. I felt like it was a fresh start. And during the two seven-month seasons I was there, I could see myself growing closer to God and learning to trust him more. My friendships with other women stayed pure, and I was confident there would be no more unhealthy ones.

Then I moved to Israel to play in a better league. My loneliness in the new location soon drove me back to a place I thought I'd never revisit. I was frustrated. I thought I had it figured out. I didn't want to be in these relationships anymore, but I didn't know how to get out.

Totally broken, I returned home for the summer. There God began speaking to my heart about contacting Athletes in Action (AIA), a ministry of Campus Crusade for Christ. I sensed that God wanted me to offer to join their fall exhibition basketball team. The team tours the country, its members sharing testimonies and playing Division I college teams.

It was risky. Several years earlier, I had been involved with AIA. But I hadn't left them on good terms, and they were aware of my struggles. Yet God kept nudging me to call. Finally, I knew I had to obey. I dialed the number, fully expecting to be turned down.

Acceptance

Amazingly, the team welcomed me, and soon I was attending the three-week pre-tour training camp. Then I realized I needed to do one more thing—confess my sinful past to the other players.

It was the scariest thing I'd ever done. I was certain my teammates would reject me. What happened instead totally awed me. Every one of them hugged me and made it clear they loved me anyway. Their reaction really brought a glimpse of God's love for me.

The tour was a great experience as well as a turning point in my battle. For the first time I realized just how important it was to have believers standing with me. Though I knew my problem would not instantly disappear, there was a way out, with my friends fighting for me and keeping me accountable.

With that in mind, I moved to AIA headquarters, where I could heal and grow in a safe Christian community. I started attending counseling and a support group. That helped me see that my unwholesome relationships began with an emotional dependency. In each case, I'd become best friends with the other woman, to the point of excluding everyone else from my life. So one aspect of my recovery was to focus on developing a number of healthy friendships.

> *For the first time, I realized just how important it was to have believers standing with me.*

I also got a part-time job with a nearby university women's basketball program, and I was thrilled to see three players and an assistant coach make commitments to Jesus. God used me. He showed me I wasn't junk.

Healing

At this point in my life, I've never felt more peace, joy, and freedom. I know the only way anyone can get out of sin is through Jesus.

Not that it's easy. I realize I may be fighting an ongoing battle for years. But I know God is the answer and that the people I was involved with are not.

> *Find someone to open up to and tell what's going on.*

For anyone struggling with same-sex temptations, I give you this advice: Find someone to open up to and tell what's going on. From personal experience I know it's impossible to break out of such relationships on your own.

For me, 1 Corinthians 6:9-11 pretty much sums things up. "Don't you know that those who do wrong will have no share in the Kingdom of God? Don't fool yourselves. Those who indulge in sexual sin, who are idol worshipers, adulterers, male prostitutes, homosexuals, thieves, greedy people, drunkards, abusers, and swindlers—none of these will have a share in the Kingdom of God. There was a time when some of you were just like that, but now your sins have been washed away, and you have been set apart for God. You have been made right with God because of what the Lord Jesus Christ and the Spirit of our God have done for you" (NLT).

I know that I used to fit in that list of the unrighteous. But now through my Savior, I'm set apart for God.

End of Search

I'm so hungry
It's not for food I long
I'm starving to find
The place where I belong

I looked in one place
And I stayed for awhile
But I felt as insecure
As a young and foolish child

So to the next spot
On I went
There I stopped
Grew even more bent

The third place I found
I wanted to stay
But the happiness ended
Lasted only a few days

I kept to myself
I was my only friend
But I found a fourth place
Where my search would end

My new friend
Had nothing missing
I could depend on him
To always be listening

He helped me eliminate all of the frauds
My new friend's name is simply God

by Barbara Mann (written at age 14)

by Jennifer A. Heck

MY FAIRY TALE

I am that girl, filthy from head to toe—not only on the outside but inside as well.

Adorned in a silk gown and precious jewels, I leaned against the stone window of the tall tower, looking out at the kingdom below, wondering when Prince Charming would arrive and sweep me off my feet. My hair was shining, my jewels shimmered, and my beauty dazzled any viewer.

I was a princess.

Really, I was a five-year-old girl who dreamed with all her heart. Yes, at a very early age my imagination captured my mind and brought me into the land of fairy tales. My wooden fort in the backyard became a castle, and a faded old nightgown transformed itself into the most lavish gown—one fit only for a princess. I hung cheap plastic pearls around my neck. After hours of play, they changed into the most rare jewels. And of course, the small tattered storybook that first sparked my love for fairy tales lay close by my side. The book did not just tell the story of

Cinderella—it also revealed the legacy of the girl I so longed to be.

Childhood Imagination

As a little girl, I easily saw myself as a princess. I ran out to my fort, slipped into the silk nightgown, and allowed my imagination to run wild. There was so much to do. Thieves and robbers were certainly not permitted in my kingdom, so I hunted them down and ensured punishment. Invitations to royal balls fought for my time as well, and I usually conceded. After all, a princess must stay busy. Still, at times when the activities lulled, I leaned out the castle window and wondered if my prince would ever come.

I waited and waited, but he never did. Doubt crept into my mind. I grew up, and one day I stared in the mirror and wondered, *Where did the beautiful princess go?* With every birthday I worked harder and harder to see the fort as a castle and the nightgown as anything but faded and outgrown. Perhaps life was just life, and maybe princesses only lived in storybooks.

> **Perhaps life was just life, and maybe princesses only lived in storybooks.**

On a summer evening when I was fifteen, my eyes were opened to what a real fairy tale is all about. I watched a Cinderella movie for the thousandth time, but this evening something caught my attention. The royal prince in his shining armor finally found Cinderella and planned to propose. However, Cinderella's appearance differed greatly. Filth and ashes covered her; tangles held fast to her hair; dirt lay beneath her fingernails. Cinderella was supposed to be elegant and beautiful, especially at such a crucial moment. Dirty clothes and messy hair were not appropriate. However, Cinderella's appearance did not seem to bother the prince. Without a moment's hesitation, he rescued her and made her his princess.

The Storybook Ending

At that moment, something happened to me. All of a sudden, I was taken aback and realized *I* am that girl, filthy from head to toe—not only on the outside but inside as well. I had tried to cover the ugliness of my state with an old faded nightgown and tarnished pearls, only serving to create a more pathetic impression. I was anything but beautiful and had no idea of the importance of the moment facing me.

There standing before me was no prince—instead, he was a King. And not just any king, but the King of kings. Jesus Christ, in the glory of his majesty and holiness, stood in stark contrast to my filth. But for some reason my state did not hinder him from coming near to me and approaching with love. Christ left his home, throne, and family to come to a distant land and find a bride, and he chose me.

There before me stood Jesus offering the chance of a lifetime—to be clean, new, and forgiven. He asked me to be his bride and enter into a royal relationship with him. At that moment I transformed into a princess. My fairy tale came true.

Jesus knew my deepest longing and desire, and he filled it. He gave me the greatest gift—my very own fairy tale. What more could a girl want? For years I thought fairy tales to be hopeless—but only because I looked in the wrong places. In Jesus, I am part of the greatest romance ever created. The only one who ever mattered chose me to be his bride. He replaced my faded and outgrown nightgown with fine linen, bright and clean. I exchanged the plastic pearls, once held tightly as treasures, for gold, silver, and truly precious stones. I am blessed with the love of not merely a handsome prince, but the most holy and beautiful King of kings and Lord of lords.

Jesus gave me the greatest gift—my very own fairy tale.

My bridegroom loves me. He chose me. I am the apple of his eye, and one day he is coming back for me. Yes, one day without any warning, the skies will roll back like a scroll, and my Prince Charming will ride out of the east on his noble white steed. He will sweep me off my feet and carry me home—just like a fairy tale. And we will live happily ever after—forever!

The best part is, my story is not just a fairy tale. It is not just a happy ending. It is my hope and my promise! It is real.

SEVENTH DAY SLUMBER | JOSEPH ROJAS

BEATING ADDICTIONS, FINDING GOD

By the time I was twelve I felt so worthless I didn't think there was a reason for me to be alive.

I closed my eyes and pictured myself sitting with my father in a boat in the middle of a blue lake. I could feel the balmy wind across my face and hear nature singing all around us. It was a day made for fishing, with nothing to hurry us.

I held my pole over the water, waiting for the perfect catch as my father and I chatted about sports. Finally, something tugged at my line. With my father's help, I pulled a fish from the water. When I looked up, I saw my father beaming with pride at me. I couldn't stop the smile from spreading over my face.

Suddenly, someone knocked into me, jolting me from my thoughts. I pulled my eyes open and saw the familiar crowds passing me by at school. Drawing in a deep breath, I pushed myself from the wall and made my way to class. But the sweet memory of the daydream lingered in my mind.

Never Fitting In

My only real memories of my father were of him beating my mother. He left when I was three, and my mother had to start working two jobs to make ends meet. I'd never known what it was like to have a father figure in my life.

I'd grown up the fat kid, never getting picked for any teams. I never had anyone teach me how to throw a football or catch a baseball. I never felt like I fit in.

By the time I was twelve I felt so worthless I didn't think there was a reason for me to be alive. I was tired of hurting. I wanted the pain to go away. Ending my life seemed a good option. Then I wouldn't have to endure what my life had become.

I pushed the thought to the back of my mind. With time, I found a group of people I fit in with. We were all misfits who joined together, needing acceptance. We found it in drugs, alcohol, and getting in trouble with the law. We figured if we didn't fit in with the cool kids, we'd see how bad we could be.

Desperate for Drugs

By fourteen, I tried my first line of cocaine. By fifteen or sixteen, I was selling drugs. By eighteen, I'd been in and out of jail. By twenty, I was a felon.

I went to jail, but got out in six months. Back at home, my cocaine addiction just got more and more out of control. Before I knew it, I had a four hundred- to five hundred-dollar-a-day habit. I smoked it, snorted it, and popped pills. I also drank heavily, doing anything to numb the pain.

I became so desperate for drugs I even stole from my mom. It broke her heart. She worked so hard to give us things. She wanted so desperately to help me. A few years before, she'd starting going to church and had given her life to Jesus. She'd tried numerous times to get me to go to church, and she told me that God could change my life. I told her there was no God. I didn't want to hear the truth.

As guilt pounded at me, I looked in the mirror and saw a reflection of someone I hated.

Man, you are worthless. Absolutely worth nothing at all. People have told you that, and that's who you are. You're a drug addict. You stole from your own mom, you loser.

Plans to Die

That's when I decided to take my life. I got enough cocaine to stop my heart and decided that this time there was no going back.

The plan was that I'd OD while my mom was at work. My brother would come home and find me dead. My body would be gone before my mother ever made it home.

I did the cocaine and my heart began beating faster and faster. The end was in sight, and I didn't care. That's how much I hated myself.

Then the door opened. My mother! She'd come home early. The last thing I wanted was for her to see this. But things were already in motion. I couldn't reverse time.

More Powerful than Addiction

I dropped to my knees as the drugs took over my body. My life began to slip away. My mother screamed and cried out to God to save my life. Miraculously, an ambulance arrived.

As the paramedics tried to save my life, I felt this unexplainable power. I knew I was experiencing God. I can't explain it, but I just knew Jesus Christ was alive. I knew he was seated at the right hand of the Father.

Suddenly, I didn't want to die.

"Jesus, save me," I cried out.

And I meant it. I decided I wasn't going back.

God is so much more powerful than any addiction.

It hasn't always been smooth sailing since I gave my life to Jesus. The bottom line is that I have to fight. Drug addiction is a powerful thing.

Cocaine was my life. It was everything to me. The devil loves that kind of addiction. It's powerful. But God is so much more powerful than any addiction.

Crazy Enough to Believe

We serve a powerful God, and I think if we ever truly get it down in our spirits how powerful our God is then we can overcome anything. When I read Philippians 4:13, I am just crazy enough to believe I can do all things through Christ who strengthens me.

It's like when a dad says, "Son, on your birthday we're taking you to Chucky Cheese." If it's a little kid, he doesn't worry about how he's getting there or if his family has enough money. He just knows that Daddy says he's going to Chucky Cheese on Friday, so he'll be there.

That's the reassurance I have when I read that Scripture. It says you can do all things through Christ. When I read that verse, that is it. I don't worry about all the rest. I just know that Daddy said it. That is it, and that is enough for me.

When I accepted Christ, I felt for the first time in my life like I'd been picked. For the first time I knew the love of a Father I'd longed for my entire life. Finally, I felt accepted—and knew I'd never go back to my old way of living.

by Cindy Ooms

"I NEED SOME HELP HERE!"

I sat in my house staring at a list of phone numbers of potential employers.

Twenty-five applications. Countless follow-up calls. One interview. My search for a summer job was not looking good. Some had all the staff they needed, and some simply did not want to hire just for the summer.

One Tuesday morning after our youth group prayer meeting, I sat in my house staring at a list of phone numbers of potential employers. "God, I really need some help here. I don't think I have many more leads to follow. I know you're in control, and I'm OK with that, but I just need to know if there's something more that I should be doing."

I walked back to my room and tossed the phone numbers onto my desk. And then the phone rang. It was our local grocery store, asking me to come in for an interview in two days. Thank you, God!!

Less than twenty seconds later, literally, the phone rang again. My best friend informed me she had landed a job for me at the catering company where she worked. After two and a half weeks of a crazy and fruitless job search, this was a total jackpot for me. I was completely blown away!

"You're in control."

What did I learn? Obviously, God's timing is perfect, and he is definitely in control. But then I started to wonder how long he had been waiting for that prayer. It's not like I hadn't been praying about my job, because I had been . . . a lot. And I had been totally believing he was going to work it out. OK, well, maybe not totally. I was starting to get a little stressed about the whole thing because I had bills to pay and no job to pay them with, and I didn't have time to run all over town filling out five job applications a day!

It takes a lot of guts to get to where you can really accept whatever God has planned.

So what was different about this latest conversation with God? At that moment, the faith element was definitely there. My whole youth group had prayed with me that morning, knowing that finding a job was a huge need. I walked away from that prayer meeting choosing to believe God was in control. Notice—that was definitely a choice. Even though there was still an element of doubt in the back of my mind, I made the decision to say, "God, I know you're in control."

Second, I was starting to realize there was a possibility I would not be able to find a job. And you know what? I was OK with that too. I really thought it out and decided if God chose not to find me a job this summer, he'd work something else out. I may not be able to go to the college I had picked out, but even if that happened, he'd lead me somewhere else. Yeah, that was not my idea of an ideal situation, but that's not the point.

A Step of Humility

It takes a lot of guts to get to where you can really accept whatever God has planned. It also takes humility. It means admitting you don't have it all figured out. It means admitting you have no idea what's going on or what's best for you. It means being OK with not having things work out your way or in your timing. And you know what? God responds to that.

When I admitted I needed God's help—desperately—and I was willing to take whatever he gave me, it was like he smiled and said, "Here you go."

I didn't get a job at the grocery store or the catering place. I actually ended up with a telemarketing job. And guess what? I'm making the money I need, but even better than that, I absolutely love my job! I have had incredible opportunities to shine a light in a dark environment.

Something as mundane as a summer job search turned into a cool opportunity for some major growth in my life. The experience really deepened my belief in the power of prayer.

And it humbled me too, which is exactly what God had in mind.

by Alyssa Franks

REAL FEAR

It is because of this immense fear of God that I can go on.

Have you ever been paralyzed with such fear that you can hear your heart pounding inside your head and your body is covered with goose bumps from head to toe? Have you experienced something so powerful it causes fear and awe to sweep through your heart and soul?

For me, this is an everyday occurrence. In fact, it is not just fear pursuing me day after day but also a longing for the peace that washes over me with intense continuity, the awe that completely consumes me, and the love that captures my heart with great fervor.

What is it that instills such fear in me? It is thinking about the creator of the universe, who is the very source of life, that gives me such a mixture of emotion—my Lord Jesus Christ. He is the Savior of my soul and the only one who can generate such fear in my heart and such loyalty as well. It is because of this immense fear of him that I can go on.

We are only his creation, and yet God sent his Son to die for us. But that is not where the story starts. To find the beginning, we must look back to the creation of all things.

Gift of Life

Genesis 1:1 says, "In the beginning God created the heavens and the earth." And he created not only the heavens and the earth but also humanity and the entire world around us. At the point of creation God knew what we would be and that we would sin against him.

Acts 17:26 explains, "From one man he made every nation of men, that they should inhabit the whole earth; and he determined the times set for them and the exact places where they should live." God is omniscient. From creation on we can see his amazing power and love. The best example of his infinite love is his ultimate sacrifice of his Son.

In John 3:16 we read, "For God so loved the world that he gave his one and only Son, that whoever believes in him shall not perish but have eternal life." God gave his Son, Jesus, for us so we might be saved through his death on the cross. Just as many saw in Mel Gibson's movie *The Passion of the Christ,* the death of Christ was vicious, evil, brutal, and painful beyond our reasoning. The Lamb of God laid down his immortality to give us new life. It is because of this miraculous gift of life that we are able to know him so intimately.

Word of God

God gave us his Word, the Bible, to read so that we might know him and his will. So for generations we have read the Bible to learn all we can about our God and maker. The message never changes, but the way it is put on our hearts does. In fact, it is called the living Word, and it speaks to all of us each time we read it. In Hebrews 4:12 we see how God uses his Word to penetrate the heart: "For the word of God is living and active. Sharper than any double-edged sword, it penetrates even to dividing soul and spirit, joints and marrow; it judges the thoughts and attitudes of the heart."

> **There is nothing in this world that could be more divine or more scary.**

In fact, it was through the Bible and God's message to me that I was called to him and answered. The very fact he knows my heart and still called out my name amazes me. Since becoming a Christian I have had many fearful and divine experiences in my life. As I mentioned before, they happen every day.

For example, the very fact I am alive and breathing this morning gives me true joy. Every time I open up the Bible I see something new. I read his message and am opened up to a new awe, fear, or pure humility every day. He is the all-powerful, almighty God of the universe, and yet he speaks to me intimately. There is nothing in this world that could be more divine—or more frightening.

It is scary for me when I think of those who will experience God's full wrath. And it is divine when I think of how he speaks to me through his Word, prayer, or instruments of his choosing. God is everything, and we are his creation. He is the meaning of divine, the reason for fear, the ultimate peace, and the source of joy.

The only fear left in me now is the fear of not having this great joy.

The Nightmare Before My Baptism

The darkness of the eerie night rests heavily upon my mind. The air is thick and smells of rotten trash. As my body slumps to the damp ground, my mind slips into confusion. I cannot move and I cannot speak. The fear of death begins to overwhelm me. I can hear distant voices, but my screams are lost in my mind. Insanity fills me as reality leaves me.

Suddenly, in a soft but clear voice I hear the words, "Are you ready?" I begin to panic as my consciousness starts to fade. A small tear rolls down my cheek as the word "help" escapes my lips in an almost silent whisper.

I awoke with a start and sat straight up in my bed, safe. "A nightmare," I say to myself with relief. My pulse races as I struggle to contemplate the dream. It all comes to me as I begin to concentrate.

I realize that I am not ready for death and that without Christ I never will be. The words "Are you ready?"

repeat in my mind. Only Christ can save me from death.

I lay back down having made the decision to fully commit my life to Christ. It was this night that I decided to be baptized because God had spoken to me through the most realistic nightmare.

by Kristy M. Rotramel (written at age 17)

by Dalan Edwin Decker

AWAY FROM THE WINDOW

No matter what they do, it seems like they're batting against a window of their own sin.

He was desperate. And blind too.

The little green housefly had been trying to get outside for three weary weeks. Night and day he buzzed around the window in my bedroom, batting against the glass. Sometimes he landed on the slick surface and ran up and down, searching for a way to reach the vision of outdoors and beyond.

I found the little pest annoying but intriguing. His sheer determination to get past that glass seemed endless. Normally, I detest flies. Ten people live in my house, and I get the job of handling the trash. On summer days with bulging trash bags, I'm not on speaking terms with these buzzing creatures. But somehow, I never could smash this little guy. Blindly, tenaciously, he launched himself at my window. I waited to see if he'd quit or die flying.

The glass wouldn't let the fly through. He was doing his best, but his best simply didn't cut it. He was doing the wrong thing.

Perfection Demanded

Sometimes that's how people act. They know that there's a heaven, and they're afraid of hell. The Ten Commandments shows them where they've messed up, so they try to do better and clean up their act. But no matter what they do, it seems like they're batting against a window of their own sin. They see that vision of life and heaven out there, but they can't seem to reach it. They're stuck.

We're all familiar with the Ten Commandments. We know the things God demands: those "thou shalt nots." No taking his name in vain. No murder or envy or stealing. No adultery. We know God says that breaking just one of the rules is the same as breaking all of them.

We also see his "thou shalts." Love me with all your heart and mind and strength. Honor your parents the same as you honor me. Sanctify a day of rest, and shut out everything in the world but me.

Rules, rules, rules! Nobody can follow them! God won't be satisfied with the best we can do either. He demands perfection.

Aaron had two sons that found out this truth about God too late. Nadab and Abihu decided to buy some favor with God by burning incense in front of the Tabernacle. They thought it was a brilliant idea, but it was a lousy one. God had a strict rule about incense: only the High Priest was allowed to burn it. So the Lord sent fire from the sanctuary and burned them to a crisp (Leviticus 10:2). Their service didn't meet his standards.

So what can we do?

Freedom Discovered

That fly hit my window for weeks. He never noticed the chance I gave him to escape: I left my bedroom door wide open. If he had thought to check, he could have gone through the door and upstairs. Our homeschool's on summer break right now, and with seven kids tearing in and out, the back door swings wide every minute or two. That fly could have slipped through somehow. He never did try.

Finally, I decided it was time for a little grace. Carefully catching the little guy in a cup, I took him outside. He hesitated at the lip of the cup, obviously not believing his own good luck. Then he took off and vanished—right into one of the big black sacks of trash in the garage. He made it to fly heaven, I guess.

I surrendered my life to Jesus, and I let him take me away from the window to real life beyond.

God did the same for me. When I was fourteen, I realized I'd never get past those Ten Commandments, or the other many rules, for that matter. My head was splitting from hitting the glass. I couldn't ignore my sins or take glass cleaner to them and hope God would let me pass. So I asked God to take over. I surrendered my life to Jesus, and I let him take me away from the window to real life beyond. Someday, when I die, I'll be free from sin. The glass will be gone for good, and I'll be in heaven—people heaven, that is!

Stuck at the Window?

Where are you? Senselessly beating at your sins? Squirting a little glass cleaner of good deeds on them to make you look better? Come on, you're smarter than that! You'll never score enough good deeds to make up for the smudges and bad marks.

Paul says that the commandments are a teacher, a schoolmaster: "The law was our guardian and teacher to lead us until Christ came" (Galatians 3:24, *NLT*). God's rules are meant to give us a lesson—and a hard one—about our own futility.

Our heavenly Father wrote the lesson for us. Only he can show us the love between the lines of his commandments. They're the final test, and we flunk every time. That's the whole idea with them. God put them on the test to show us how totally helpless we are. We're like a kid in kindergarten who's given a trigonometry exam. There's no way we can pass it, much less ace it!

We're like a kid in kindergarten who's given a trigonometry exam.

That's where Christ comes in. He lived a perfect life, keeping all of God's commandments to the letter. He paid the price for every one of our sins when he passed the biggest test of all, on Calvary. All we have to do is claim the power and forgiveness of the blood he shed on that old rugged cross. When we do, we quit making a mess of our lives and allow Jesus to score an A+ for us.

The other option isn't so cool, you know. It's called fire. The people who try to work their way around the glass only earn heartache in this world and judgment in the life to come. Nadab and Abihu found that out the hot way.

Oh, yeah—the little fly had a name. I called him Dalan, after me. Maybe there's a fly with your name buzzing against a window somewhere. It won't make the world a better place to crunch one fly, and the bug sure could use a hand.

It helps everyone to get away from that window.

by Lacquen Davis

FACING MY FEARS

It's been a whole year that we've been planning this mission trip. Now I'm not sure I want to go.

Thursday, July 7

It's the night before my first mission trip. I can't believe it! Tomorrow morning I'm going with my dad and seven other people from my church to Ecuador. I'm the only teenager with this group of adults.

Ecuador!! I don't even know how to speak the language or what the culture or people will be like! Just being in a foreign country will be scary. But beyond that, the thing that totally freaks me out is giving my testimony. We practiced giving our testimonies at our church a few weeks ago, and I just did not like it. It brings up all the pain and hurt when I think about the past, and it makes me want to cry. Why would I want to stand in front of the people in Ecuador and share that?

It's been a whole year that we've been planning this mission trip. Now I'm not sure I want to go. I found out today that my sister is sick. If I leave, I won't know if she gets better or worse. I'll be in a totally different country for ten days! Is it worth it? Is it worth leaving the contact I have with my sister? Is it worth facing all these fears? I could turn back and just stay home. Will it really matter if I don't go? I'm just a teenager—what impact will I have?

But something inside me knows I have to go. I committed to this a year ago. I have done all the fundraising. I know God wants me to go. I just have to face all my fears and concerns. After all, they are just False Evidences Appearing Real (FEAR). This is something I need to do.

Tuesday, July 12

I made it! We are here in Carpuela, Ecuador, with our missionary, Yolanda. It's not at all what I thought it was going to be. I thought their houses would be like cardboard boxes. Instead, they have cities and towns like the United States.

We did a crusade yesterday, and I got to see a lot of what the village life is like. Their lifestyles are just so different from ours. Here, we have jobs and we make more money in a day than they might make in a month or year! I feel so bad for the kids. They are in ragged clothes and don't have much money. All the houses are so small and a lot don't have electricity or running water. It's just a different world here.

One of the things we're doing here is to help the Freedom Valley Christian Center with some work projects. Half our team is working on building a brick wall around an office building for security. The other half (my half!) is working on some cleaning and painting projects. Yesterday we cleaned chairs and different parts of the church. Today we get to paint! We're turning the dull gray desks into the beautiful colors of the Ecuadorian flag—red, blue, and yellow. Although my hand gets numb from having to put three coats of paint on each desk, I am happy to know this will bring smiles to the kids' faces.

Friday, July 15

My absolute favorite part of this trip so far has been spending time with the Compassion International kids. It was hard to interact with them, though, because of the language barrier. I wish I knew more Spanish! They would point at me and say stuff, but I didn't know what they wanted. I just played patty-cake and some kind of circle game with them. They are so cute and loveable! It makes me so sad to know how poor their families are. I will definitely remember the kids for a long time. It's going to be hard to say good-bye.

It's almost the end of the trip, and I've realized that I haven't had the fear I thought I would! God has been with me during this trip. We performed our skits, prayed with people, interacted with people, and did our work . . . all of that without any fear! Fear definitely is False Evidences Appearing Real! And as far as my testimony, I didn't end up having to give it. That was a relief for me. But I was ready to do it and will do it anytime God wants me to. God took my mind off a lot of things. He showed me that things aren't always as bad as I make them seem and that I shouldn't have fear.

Sunday, July 17

These past ten days have really flown by. We are already on our way home. I miss the kids! I will miss everything about Ecuador. (Well, everything but the food—I love my American food!) Being in Ecuador was such a fun and exciting experience. I've grown closer to God during this trip because everything was centered around him. Because of this it was easy to get to know him better, without the normal distractions of life. And I'm kind of glad I was the only teenager on our team. I think if other teens had gone, it would've been cool, but I would have been more distracted. This way, my focus stayed closer to God.

I will definitely remember the kids for a long time. It's going to be hard to say good-bye.

Another neat thing was hearing our missionary's testimony. Yolanda hasn't always lived a Christian life—especially during her childhood and teen years. It made me see that people don't have to have lived perfect lives in the past to be used by God.

I didn't really see myself as a missionary these past ten days, but I know we were like missionaries in some way. Although we didn't learn the language and spend a lot of time there, we did show the people of Ecuador the love of Jesus. That was the most important thing. We represented Jesus by the stuff we did and the love we showed.

I'm ready to go on more mission trips. I would absolutely love to go back to Ecuador! But I'm also ready to go anywhere. Well, let me clarify: most anywhere. I think if I had to go on a mission trip to Iraq, I just might cry. But even if I did, God would be with me and he would take away any of my fears.

Fulfilled

As my eyes are closed
My heart aches.
Pain and confusion run through my head.
My lips move, but no words are spoken.
Tears run down my tarnished face.
As I grow courage and strength,
My whimpers turn into words.
And I speak,
"You know my heart, Lord,
Please lift this heavy burden,
I can't carry it alone.
Just fill me with your strength
and warmth."

by Samantha Locke (written at age 15)

by Tekoa Miller

WONDERFUL COUNSELOR

I knew I had to make a decision soon, but I had no idea what to do next.

It was December of my senior year, my last year in high school. Everyone was asking me where I was headed after graduation in May. What college would I go to? Had I been accepted? What would I study? Where would I work? The questions were overwhelming.

Worries

I worried day after day about what my future would hold. I wasn't sure how to answer any of the questions people asked, and yet I knew that sometime I would have to answer them. I decided to take action. I looked into colleges, researched the job market, estimated tuition costs, read up on different occupations, and thought about what I wanted to study. I knew I had to make a decision soon, but I had no idea what to do next.

Why wouldn't God tell me what to do? Why didn't he drop a billboard outside my window with instructions for my future? Why wasn't he giving me advice?

It was then I realized I had never asked God for help. I never paused to see what he might have to say.

Trust

I felt God gently remind me of Isaiah 9:6: "And he will be called Wonderful Counselor, Mighty God, Everlasting Father, Prince of Peace." God is my Wonderful Counselor, and he is willing to help me whenever I ask. I just have to stop and humble myself to ask him. Instead, I had thought I could do it myself and had tried logically to figure out where to go next.

After that revelation, I still didn't see a billboard with my name on it. God didn't speak out loud and tell me where I should attend college. I just had to learn to trust my counselor, knowing he wouldn't lead me astray.

LOOK WHAT I CAN DO!

"... I urge you to live a life worthy of the calling you have received."

—Ephesians 4:1

by Meryl Herran

I FELT LIKE A LOSER

"So? What did you get on the SAT?"

As soon as I stepped into my first class, I wished I'd stayed home from school. It's not like I would've had to fake being sick. My stomach twisted uncomfortably as I listened to everybody else comparing SAT scores.

No Comparison

My friend Mindy was way too bubbly.

"So? What did you get on the SAT?" she asked in a high-pitched squeal.

Before I had a chance to dodge the question, she continued her annoying chatter.

"I did awesome!" Mindy said as she blurted out her score. "How did you do?"

"Not that well," I said softly as I glanced up at the clock, hoping the teacher would get the class started.

"Oh, whatever. I know you did great," she insisted.

Mindy's broad, cheery smile only made me feel worse.

I remained quiet and simply plopped down in my chair and unzipped my book bag. I desperately wanted to avoid anymore SAT chatter, but I couldn't escape it—not in that class or anywhere else. The buzz was the same all over school—in the hallways, the cafeteria, the parking lot. It seemed everyone was comparing scores. I was relieved when the day finally ended and I could go home and get away from it all.

Too Much Pressure

When Mom walked through the door and found me scarfing ice cream straight from the carton, she knew something was wrong. I told her all about my gloating classmates.

"So what if some of them did better?" Mom asked. "Your score is still really good."

"Not good enough," I sighed as I pitifully plunged my spoon back into the Rocky Road. "This test totally determines my future!"

"Don't put so much pressure on yourself, honey," Mom said. "I know how hard you worked to prepare, and that's all you can do."

"No!" I defiantly shook my head. "I'm gonna retake the test again. I'll improve my score even if it kills me!"

"I don't like the pressure you're putting on yourself," Mom repeated. "Promise me that you'll let God help you next time around."

"What do you mean?" I asked.

"I want you to do your best, then leave it in God's hands."

Easy for you to say, I thought, irritated by how easy she made it sound. She'd obviously forgotten what it was like to be in my shoes.

"I wanna be a veterinarian, and to do that I need the right test scores to get into college," I insisted. "It's not like praying will get me a degree."

Mom sat in silent thought for a moment, then said gently, "If you pray for the strength and courage to trust in God, and if you truly believe things will ultimately work out the way the Lord intends, you'll feel a lot better."

Sense of Peace

While I was far from convinced, I still tried to follow Mom's advice. In the weeks leading up to the exam, I talked to my friends in youth group about my testing anxieties. And each evening before bed, I read Scriptures and said a prayer that went something like this:

"If it's your will, Lord, please give me the knowledge and strength to do well on this test. But also help me remember that my life will always be OK as long as I trust and love you with all my heart and soul."

> *"If you pray for the strength and courage to trust in God, you'll feel a lot better."*

Finally, the big day arrived. Driving to the testing site, I remembered one of the verses I'd studied: "May the God of hope fill you with all joy and peace as you trust in him, so that you may overflow with hope by the power of the Holy Spirit" (Romans 15:13). As I took a deep breath and said a little prayer, a sense of peace washed over me.

When I entered the testing room, I felt different than when I took the exam the first time. This time my head didn't pound, my stomach didn't churn, and my hands didn't tremble in fear. In fact, I felt amazingly calm knowing that regardless of how I scored on this test—or any test, for that matter—my future was in the hands of a loving God I could really trust.

by Melissa Hill

HEADACHES, BUG BITES, AND HUNGER

What can I give up that's important to me? What nagging want will drive me to pray?

"We're gonna fast on Saturday. You should fast with us!" my friends said.

Pause.

"I'll pray about it," I replied.

Everyone Is Doing It

I was on a summer missions trip, and my teammates decided to fast and pray for the non-believing families who were hosting us in their homes.

My response sounds like maybe I was afraid, or I wasn't willing to give up one day's food for the sake of Christ. But that's not true.

Certainly I wasn't eager to not eat for a day. I like to eat. I don't like to be hungry. Besides, not eating sometimes sets off my migraines, and that's no fun. I paused not because of this but because I know that fasting should be something that's between me and God. I never want to fast because I've been told to or have been pressured into it. I should fast when God calls me to fast.

Too often I try to do godly things just because everyone else is and it seems like a good thing to do. I forget that God takes these things seriously. God doesn't take fasting lightly; in his eyes, it's not a spur-of-the-moment "yeah, sure" decision. It's not about who I am in the eyes of other people. I should seek to see myself as God does.

So I prayed about it. "God, I want to honor you. I want to show you how much I care about my host family and the earnestness of my prayers for them. I want to sacrifice my needs for the needs of others. My team is fasting on Saturday; is this something you want me to do?"

I waited and journaled and thought. *What can I give up that's important to me? What nagging want will drive me to pray for my host family?*

More Than I Expected

Through this prayer time God pointed out to me some things I depend on—things he wanted me to let go of for a few days. To be honest, it's not what I wanted to hear. I wanted him to say, "Oh don't worry about it. I know your heart, just eat." Instead I felt his Spirit guiding me to fast with my team that Saturday. Not only that, I also felt God pressing on me that I should also give up my bug spray, bug bite cream, and pain relievers for the weekend. My jaw dropped.

"But, God, I have like twenty-five bug bites on my legs alone! And what if I get a headache, what good am I then? I need to keep myself at my best for you. I need to make sure the itching and pain don't get in the way of my work for you."

I . . . what good am I? . . . I need . . . my work for You. . . . I stopped. Was I nuts? Who was I talking to? *"My* work for you"? What arrogance! It's only God's work in me that's able to accomplish anything. I was slapped in the face with my own stupidity.

So I sucked up my pride and my fear and said OK. "All right, I'll do it."

Wholly and Sacrificially Devoted

So how'd it turn out, you may wonder.

I told my teammates I'd fast with them, but I didn't tell them about the other things. I never told anyone. It was between me and God. I didn't want to glorify myself or appear to be trying to one-up others. My goal was to be obedient to God and show him I was wholly and sacrificially devoted to him.

So I did it. And I lived to tell about it. It wasn't easy. My legs itched and my head ached. But not nearly as bad as I'd expected. God showed me that he is the one who takes care of me. He's the one who takes away my pain and helps me push through life. Every time my bug bites itched or my head hurt, I remembered to be thankful for the awesome things God does in my life and the phenomenal opportunities he gives me.

And I remembered to pray. I prayed long and hard. I showed my heart to God and asked him to work through his power. Being vulnerable with God allowed him to work in my life and the lives of others.

LOOKING AT LIFE
THROUGH DEATH

I wanted to do something that made a difference and not just something for myself.

Numb. That's the only word to describe how I felt. Not angry at God or questioning him. Not asking, Why me? Not confused about how it all happened at once.

Numb.

Hurt Times Three

I sat in the hospital waiting room. My best friend and bandmate, Uno, was there. While on a summer European tour, he'd become ill and was diagnosed with a rare disease called Guillain Barré syndrome that left him nearly dead. Another bandmate, Joey, found out his grandfather had died, and Joey traveled home to Africa to be with his family. On top of all that, and perhaps most painful for me, my dad also was in the hospital. He'd had a heart attack.

My father had always been my support in life. I had a great family, which is starting to be rare these days. I felt my dad's strength in our family; he really led our house. He was a very good man.

My father influenced me in many ways, including musically. Growing up, my dad could pick up an instrument and, within twenty minutes, play something on it. He just had that in him.

As a kid, I always wanted to do something in the arts. Then I started getting more into music around high school. I wanted to do something that made a difference, and not just something for myself. I just felt that music could be that avenue. I owe where I am today, as a member of LA Symphony, to my dad.

When It's Time

One week after my dad went into the hospital, he passed away. In the middle of it, the numbness remained. I cried a lot, but at the same time realized my dad was never scared of death. He said, "When it's my time to go, I'm out of here. I'm going to be with the Lord." I held on to that sentiment to get me through the rough time.

Death is a part of life. That's what I learned through all of it. My father could have died ten or fifteen or twenty years from now and I would be just as hurt and sad. Death would still be part of life. I can't allow that to affect my faith in God because that's just how life works. Why would I be shaken in that sense?

During this time, the band really opened up to each other. Uno came home from the hospital almost three months later. We ended up putting a lot of our emotions on the record, saying this is what we went through. We realized that no matter what happened in life we had to keep going because God has a plan for us, and it's worth it. Through all these trials and tribulations, we're still here and going to keep going.

Musical Inspiration

Flynn made the track for "Give" (on our album *Disappear Here*) and as soon as I heard it I was like, "I have an idea for our content and chorus." He said, "Cool, write it." I wrote the chorus and verses, inspired by my father. The number one thing I thought of concerning my father was that he was a giver, someone who constantly gave to his family and to everyone around him.

No matter what happens in life, God has a plan for us, and it's worth it.

My father would hang out with some friends at McDonald's every morning. There was this homeless guy who was always there. My dad started doing all these things for this man. He helped him get a bank account. He helped him start to get his life back together; no one else was giving this guy the time of day. That's just the kind of guy my dad was.

I wrote a verse about my father, about the funeral experience. There were an extremely large number of people at my dad's funeral. I really can say that when you spend your life giving to people and investing in people's lives you're going to reap that. You could see the fruit of my father's life at his funeral by the many people who showed up. Even the pastor doing the funeral couldn't believe how many people were there.

Another song I wrote from the experience is "Pops Song," one of my favorite on the record. I actually started it before my father went to be with Jesus. It talks about the importance of a father in everyone's life. I go through scenarios where one person never had a father, another did and the parents divorced, and another had a grandfather growing up. I brought it to the guys and they liked the idea.

A Life Theme

Through the whole experience, I realized things are not going to be easy, no matter what happens in life, especially if you're going to decide to take hold of something that God wants you to do. What I've learned, and am still learning, is what a huge thing it is to never give up.

God puts things in your heart and he gives you opportunities to do something great for him. Just do it. Don't give up, no matter what. That's really the whole theme of our records.

And it was definitely the theme of my father's life.

Shared Ground

We shared this ground
You and I
We touched the same dust
Watched the same sky

Tread the same grass
On the same dirt
We shared our world
All the joy, all the hurt

We gazed up to
The same set of stars
I wish we could catch them
And put them in jars

Pleasure and pain
By both we were awed
Only one major difference:
You are God

by Tekoa Miller (written at age 17)

by Dalene V. Parker

STEP OUT AND BE SEEN

God spoke to me through that clerk and that gas pump.

A bitter night wind bit through my thin jacket as I tried for the third time to get the gas pump to do its duty. I had already pressed the "Pay Inside" button several times, and when the screen failed to allow me to proceed, I pressed the "Help" button several times as well.

I expected a friendly voice to boom over the speaker and give me some direction. From where I stood shivering, I could see the clerk inside, warm and toasty, drinking her soda and reading some charts. But she did not seem to notice my difficulty until I finally gave up and stepped inside.

Irritable Salesclerk

"Ma'am, I'd like to get some gas if you'd please turn on the pump," I said as politely as I could between chattering—and partially gritted—teeth.

"Well, you have to step out and be seen," she answered, as though I should have known better. "I'm not turning the pump on for nobody I can't see."

"Why didn't you tell me that when I pressed the 'Help' button, then?" I asked in return. "I would have been glad to step out if I'd known that was the problem."

"I can't leave my post by the cash register to come out there," was her reply.

"Don't you have an intercom?"

"No."

"Oh, I see. Well, would you please turn the pump on for me now that you've seen me?"

"Yes."

"Thank you."

Nagging Discouragement

My first inclination was to get irritated. Make that more irritated. After all, I was in a hurry and very cold. Besides, this lady had no reason to be suspicious of me. And she certainly didn't go out of her way to be of any assistance. But my second impulse was to thank her for helping me realize something rather important.

You see, I had been asked to speak at our school's First Priority meeting the next day. First Priority is a group of teens who meet once a week during lunch to share their faith and encourage one another to live godly lives. But this was not a week I felt worthy of sharing anything with anybody. In fact, I would much rather have not been at school at all.

Bummed out all week, I didn't really think I could provide much inspiration. Nothing really bad had happened, but a lot of little things were nagging at me, and I was weighed down with a heaviness I couldn't quite explain. It felt almost like a lead shawl had wrapped around my shoulders and a bucket of beans had been poured upside down on my head.

In spite of that, God spoke to me through that clerk and that gas pump.

Spiritual Fuel Tank

First, I was cold because I wasn't properly clothed. Physically, I hadn't worn my heavy jacket on a cold night; spiritually, I hadn't spent enough time putting on "the full armor of God" (Ephesians 6:11) or basking in the warmth of fellowship with him.

Second, I not only needed to ask for help at the gas pump, I also needed to come inside to get it. Coming inside spiritually meant I needed to get back into God's Word, come into his presence, sit at his feet, and pay attention to his directions. Part of his directions were for me to "step out and be seen" at First Priority by sharing this story.

God showed me that I didn't have to feel particularly spiritual or strong in order to have an opportunity for impact. As soon as I came inside for his help, he was more than willing to turn on the pump of his incredible love and forgiveness, wrapping me in his warmth. And he was ready to fill my spiritual fuel tank with all I needed to get through the challenges I had been trying to face while basically running on empty.

I didn't have to feel particularly spiritual or strong in order to have an opportunity for impact.

When I emerged from the gas station after paying my bill, I was in for a pleasant surprise. At the pump next to where I had parked was Martha, one of my best buddies from a school I used to go to. We hadn't talked in months. After a quick hug and a little chatter, we made plans for a catch-up walk and talk the next Saturday.

From that moment, things started looking better. It was as though God had been waiting to fill me up so I could step out and be seen for him, no matter what my feelings or failures.

I'm amazed God can speak through gas pumps and ornery salesclerks.

I'm even more amazed he can speak through me.

by Ashley Hayes

ROCK ON!

Because of my garb I was considered a freak and scorned by the "godly" kids at my school.

"Are you a vampire?"
"No."
"Do you worship vampires?"
"No."
I was tired of this.
"Are you friends with vampires?"
"No."
My voice sounded flat and I clenched my teeth a little.
"I have a question for you. If you really think I am a vampire, why are you trying to aggravate me?"
This dialogue took place at least three times a week during my eighth grade year. Sometimes I walked to my next class with my fists balled, other times I blinked the tears out of my eyes, always trying to forget what had just happened.
Even though I wore a large cross around my neck, talked about my involvement at church, read my Bible in school, and tried my best to lead a Christian life, still

I was perceived as some kind of Satanist or cult member. Why? Because I liked a band called the Smashing Pumpkins. I wore a Smashing Pumpkins T-shirt—usually black—and jeans every day. Because of my garb I was considered a "freak" and scorned by the "godly" kids at my school.

Meeting Jesus and Loving Music

I accepted Christ toward the end of my sixth grade year. Then before I entered seventh grade, I discovered the Smashing Pumpkins. I fell in love with their music. For the first time I actually *felt* something while listening to music. I was amazed that the lead singer, Billy Corgan, could capture such personal feelings in songs and broadcast them on the radio. I often experienced those same feelings and found it comforting to know I wasn't alone.

Billy's lyrics were complicated sometimes, abstract at other times, and occasionally clear as windows. Sometimes he wrote about beautiful things; other times he wrote about stuff most of us have a hard time admitting. I respected that and I hooked onto it. The disturbing lyrics were the ones I loved the most because they were so honest.

The first line in my favorite song was, "The world is a vampire." Curious people would ask me why I liked it, and I answered them truthfully, "Because I feel that way!" I felt like the world wanted to suck the life out of me or make me dead like it was. I felt that every moment of every day, and the song talked about the constant fight to simply try to be alive—not just physically, but also emotionally and spiritually.

Praising God for Making Rock

I always felt like my church accepted both sides of me. The three other kids attending my youth group believed me when I said I loved Jesus. However, when our youth group did a series on music, I was a little bothered by it. I felt like the music I listened to was frowned upon simply because it didn't conform to the church. Our teacher said the one thing she would probably change about me was the kind of music I liked. I wasn't offended. I think she feared I would get wrapped up in the world of rock and fall away from Christ. She wanted what she thought was best for me.

> *Slowly, more people have learned to stop scorning me and to accept me as I am.*

People had a hard time seeing that I didn't like rock for the image, though my black band T-shirts and experiments with black and silver makeup certainly contributed to that idea. I liked the honesty of rock because there are no rules, and it's whatever you want it to be. Slowly, more people have learned to stop scorning me and to accept me as I am.

Setting New Standards

At one point, I felt God convicting me to start censoring what I listened to. I wondered if I should stop listening to rock completely. I thought about taking people's advice and listening only to Christian music. But through prayer and meditation I reached a conclusion.

In Philippians 4:8, Paul tells us: "Finally brothers, whatever is true, whatever is noble, whatever is right, whatever is pure, whatever is lovely, whatever is admirable—if anything is excellent or praiseworthy think about such things."

This set the standard by which I judge music and other things. I do have to guard what I listen to, and there is a lot of music I'm sure Christ doesn't want me to hear. So when I first hear a song, I ask myself: *Is this pure, lovely, praiseworthy, or excellent? Does it make me feel like talking to my heavenly Father?* If the answer is no, I ban it from my musical diet.

This meant giving up some Smashing Pumpkins songs and others by musicians I enjoyed. But I experienced the joy of knowing I pleased my heavenly Father. I don't want to misuse the incredible gift of music the Lord has given me.

For the songs that I can say, "Yes, this is praiseworthy, excellent, pure, or lovely," I sit back, crank up the volume, and enjoy some rock with my Father in heaven.

by Jason

STORMS RAGE, GOD CONQUERS

That night, I knew my mom was an alcoholic.

Growing up in rural Ohio required creative thinking. Despite the isolation, I never minded not having access to movie theatres and shopping malls. My formula for fun featured my red bicycle and a few mischievous buddies.

A perfect afternoon entailed cruising downtown and picking up a few essentials prior to battle—bubblegum, sunflower seeds, and chocolate milk. Clad in full armor (actually, old baseball equipment), we headed for Sherwood Forest (OK, the local elementary school playground). Slaying dragons, building fortresses, and rescuing damsels in distress could all be accomplished before the evening dinner bell rang.

Little did I know that a real life battle brewed within my family, featuring obstacles far greater than the villains from a childhood fairy tale.

My Mom's Secret

At the age of thirteen, my already complex world of pimples, relationships, and low self-confidence would be challenged all the more when my mother's behavior began changing. A once upbeat and highly supportive mother became withdrawn and inattentive to my needs. Seeing Mom cry over ordinary events became commonplace. In an effort to cope, she left with friends, often returning in the morning's early hours.

The problem's mystery cleared one evening when a police officer arrived at our house with my mom at his side. I initially assumed she was in a car accident or perhaps was helping him find someone. Within seconds, I realized the cop had arrested my mother for reckless driving while intoxicated.

That night, I knew my mom was an alcoholic.

The following months were rough. I felt terribly sorry for my mother, while at the same time feeling equally embarrassed by her crime. Keeping secrets in a small town was impossible, and Mom's habit quickly leaked. I could feel eyes blanketing me every time I left the house—at least that's what my thoughts told me. Mom tried counseling, with little success. Alcohol became her primary love.

In an effort to pry my mother's grip away from negative influences, my father took a new job in another part of the state. Sadly, alcoholism is a disease, not something you can just leave behind at your old house for the next owner to deal with. Within months, Mom stumbled again. Another driving while intoxicated charge sentenced her to three months in prison and years of house arrest.

An already rocky marriage became rockier, and my dad's outlet became his new career. My brother left early for college, and now I lived at home with an alcoholic . . . and now a workaholic.

A New Start

For whatever reason, bitterness never consumed me. In spite of my limited understanding of God, I felt like someone watched over me, protecting me from my painful circumstances. Although the move was intended to help my mom, it actually was a bigger help to me. I met a group of wonderful friends that took me to a Youth for Christ meeting.

For the first time, I began to understand that God had a plan for me. The words of Jeremiah 29:11, 13 struck a chord. "'For I know the plans I have for you,' declares the Lord, 'plans to prosper you and not to harm you, plans to give you hope and a future. . . . You will seek me and find me when you seek me with all your heart.'" Rather than hold God accountable for my family crisis, I trusted his promise and committed my life to him. And at fifteen, I began walking by faith.

Little did I know, the next four years of high school would become the best years of my life. I gave football a whirl my freshman year and ended up team captain prior to graduation. I applied myself academically and made the National Honor Society. I helped start a Students Against Drunk Driving (SADD) chapter at my school and membership grew. I became a student leader in my Youth for Christ group and started giving my faith away. And I was fortunately surrounded by godly friends that became like family. While storms raged at home, God sent just enough encouragement to keep my morale afloat.

One More Roadblock

With high school winding down, I faced one more roadblock. College came knocking, and with all the troubles, my family could only offer limited financial assistance. Fearing massive debt or no college at all, I prayed. My youth leader also prayed. We jointly believed in God's provision.

I did my part and met with guidance counselors to discuss scholarship opportunities. My grades were good but not good enough. I was athletic but not a standout. Finally we discovered one scholarship designed to help students coming from troubled family backgrounds. I knew I'd been dealt a bad hand, but I wasn't homeless or starving. I convinced myself that my story didn't contain enough drama to win.

While storms raged at home, God sent just enough encouragement to keep my morale afloat.

On the eve of the scholarship submission deadline, my youth leader called to check the progress of my search. I told him about the scholarship and my doubts. He immediately summoned me to his house. After a late night of writing and proofreading, we produced a final copy, but I mailed it out with nagging doubt.

Two months later I received a phone call from a foundation representative with the news that I had been granted a four-year scholarship that covered tuition, housing, and book fees at any public or private university within the state. I was speechless. God really did have a plan for me.

I recently appointed myself chairman of the Don't Doubt God committee. The blessings and protection he has given me extend beyond my wildest imaginations. So often young Christians wonder if ongoing faithfulness ever translates into blessings. They cash in their spiritual chips before God has time to reward them. I am living proof that, although not easy, following Christ is the best choice anyone can ever make.

Life at home is still a struggle, but together the Lord and I have slain several real-life dragons. And he's reassured me that good guys can finish first.

Never Really Alone

Once there was only sorrow that kept me in the dark, cold and all alone
Once my heart was formed into nothing but a pit that was filled with rocky stone
And nobody could reach me through my stony wall
Nobody could help me up whenever I did fall
Because the stone was blocking them from seeing who I was inside
The smile I wore was only a mask used so that my sorrow could hide
Until it finally ate me up and I became cold and uncaring
My feelings were a mystery that I didn't feel like sharing
And that mystery even began to become hard for me to understand
I started to push away what had become a part of a plan
That plan was love, and I pushed it away because I thought it would fix it all
But instead it only thickened the stone on my wall
Until finally it was no longer keeping people out but keeping me in
My life became a dark place filled with lies and sin

And everyone tried to help me, but they
  couldn't get through
Because the barricade had made me believe
  that no one was true
So I sat all alone to dwell in my pain
  with no one to care
I started to wonder if God was even really
  there
But then a tiny crack began to appear in
  my cage of stone
I began to hear voices whispering to me,
  telling me that I was not alone
And slowly my stony wall finally did
  began to crumble
I was a little shaky at first and a few
  times I did stumble
But in the end I got up and opened my
  eyes to see
That the only thing that was in my way of
  loving people was me
And all I had to do was open up and stop
  being blind
Once I couldn't see a thing, but the Lord
  fixed it with people who are kind
And now everything is fine, now I understand
That I was never really alone because God
  always had my hand

by Sharecia Blake (written at age 14)

THE MUSIC ON MY HEART

I began to realize the bleakness of the lifestyle I was living.

Chico State University was once dubbed the number one party school in the nation. When I received a soccer scholarship to attend there, I seemed to fit right into the lifestyle the school offered.

I admit—I was a mess. Even though I grew up around Christianity and had seen it from afar, I'd never really formed a relationship with God. I'd even gotten into some drugs in high school, and starting college I had no idea what I wanted to do with my life. I thought maybe I would write screenplays or get into film.

My freshman year, I hit rock bottom.

My Mission

Steadily, I began to realize the bleakness of the lifestyle I was living. I began to understand that there had to be more to life. There wasn't any one event that opened my eyes. Somehow, God got hold of my heart. I felt drawn by his grace and his life, and something began to click in my head. I felt like God really met me.

After accepting Christ, I suddenly felt like I had something before me to work at—music and writing. Even though I was an English Literature major, I got involved in the local music scene. I became somewhat of a closet musician, teaching myself to play the guitar, piano, and harmonica. I would sneak into the school of music at Chico State at two in the morning and play the piano for hours.

My Music

As a teen, I'd been involved in hip-hop culture. So I began writing songs that combined my love of that style with my love of folk, along with other musical influences. I also started studying poetry and keeping a personal journal. Somehow, all of these things seemed to come together in my songs.

Around this time I met Robert Marvin, a music producer. I decided to travel to Nashville with him for the summer. We moved to the Christian music capital, literally sleeping in the back of his truck as we journeyed across the country.

Though my plan had been to only live there for three months, Toby McKeehan (aka TobyMac) had heard my stuff and encouraged me to stay. He said he really thought I could make it as a musical artist. So I stayed. It took me four years to produce my first album. I didn't want to back down from the original, eclectic style I felt God had given me.

My Gift

Getting started in music was probably the easiest thing in the world for me. But really carving a name for myself and not just being a novelty has been a whole lot of work. Really the way I got into music felt like a gift, almost like it was just something I slipped into that's ended up being really fun.

I try to be very honest and real through my music and my life.

I feel like God is using me and my music, both with Christians and non-Christians. I try to be very honest and real through my music and my life. A lot of my music and what I do deals with the harsh reality of the world. I try not to pull any punches. Also, in light of that, I want to show the grace and the hope that exists within the world. I always find myself trying to really identify with people where they are in the middle of their junk, but also help them, without being preachy, see the grace and hope that God has for them. I wasn't called to be a preacher but a musician.

My Time with God

Sometimes it's hard to believe that this college boy who didn't know what he wanted to do with his life is now doing music professionally. Traveling and doing music has been a change of pace, so it's been challenging in a lot of ways because all of this is very new and humbling.

God is constantly teaching me the importance of my daily time to seek him and find him. I talk about that in a song I wrote called "Chicago." It's about being in different cities and seeing the grace of God there in what he's doing. You find your faith has to be mobile and go with you.

Throughout being a part of this music business, I've learned that it's good to have people you're connected to who love you. If I've learned anything about my life it's that I value so much the friends I have who have stood by me continuously—it gets challenging when you're playing forty cities in fifty days.

My True Self

One of my favorite songs on my first album, *Bullet*, is a ballad on the end of the record that's called "Won't Back Down." It was the first song I ever performed the whole way through on the piano. It's about how in the midst of trials and the things of life you have to keep pressing through because there's something on the other side. That song's always been dear to me, one of my favorites. It really reflects my life and acknowledges the fact that God's in control of all things.

Through my music, most of all, I hope I've remained true to myself. I've always said that when I die, on my tombstone, they would say, "He was a man who loved humility and compassion." I also want people to say, "He wasn't swayed by what everybody thought he should do, but he really was a person of conviction."

And as a person of conviction, I'm going to continue dancing to the beat of my own drummer and making the music that God has placed on my heart.

by Tekoa Miller

UNIQUE INDIVIDUALS

It doesn't matter to God if we aren't like other people.

I have a friend named Matt. He's not like most people. He likes to wear pink shirts with yellow pants. He loves to break fashion rules and dress differently. He likes to wear the most absurd combinations of clothes. Matt loves to be different. He doesn't do anything like other people. Some people look at Matt and see a guy who needs a course in simple fashion sense. I see someone who doesn't conform to the standards of others.

The World's Rules

In this world there's a set of rules that someone made up. Those rules tell us what we can wear and when and what names should be on our clothes. The rules let us know that we have to be like everyone else to be cool.

Guess what? We don't.

God doesn't have a set of rules like that. He won't disown you just because your clothes came from a thrift store or because you don't own the latest CD. He doesn't base your worth on your stuff. He loves you just the way you are.

Peer pressure is what makes us believe those rules are true. If the most popular person in school is wearing certain clothes, then we think we all have to wear those clothes to be cool like them.

Guess what? We don't.

God's Rules

Because God doesn't base our worth on our clothing, it doesn't matter to him if we aren't like other people. In fact, God likes it when we are different. "Don't copy the behavior and customs of this world, but let God transform you into a new person by changing the way you think. Then you will know what God wants you to do, and you will know how good and pleasing and perfect his will really is" (Romans 12:2, *NLT*).

It's easier to go along with the crowd rather than be different. Being a Christian is rarely easy. But we are promised a reward: "God blesses the people who patiently endure testing. Afterward they will receive the crown of life that God has promised to those who love him" (James 1:12, *NLT*).

Before we make our decisions based on a popularity poll, we need to think about what God would like to see us do. Most likely, his view is different than our friends' opinions.

by Brian Coates

THE BAND CAMP DARE

Arthur was dared to drink the bottle of liquid Anbesol he had brought with him to camp.

When I think about peer pressure, an old school mate always comes to mind. To protect his identity, I will refer to him as Arthur. Arthur was a year or so older than me, and in high school we both played trumpet in the marching band. This is where we met, and even though our friendship never managed to make it outside the boundaries of the marching field, he has left an indelible impression on me that I doubt will ever leave. This story begins in the last few weeks of summer vacation before my sophomore year of high school.

Marching Band Practice

The marching band season had just started, with the band having daily practices at our high school. After a week or so of those sessions, we would all pack up and move onto the campus of a local college for a week of day-long practice sessions. The typical day had us waking very early in the morning, usually around 7 AM. With the exception of just a few breaks for water and meals, we spent eleven hours or so a day practicing relentlessly. Hour after hour we would stand in a grass-barren field painted with football lines, the blazingly hot sun beating down on us.

Now either Arthur was just a sucker for peer pressure or these were the perfect conditions for eroding his common sense to an unbelievably low level, making him susceptible to acts of stupidity he regularly wouldn't be interested in. But I am getting ahead of myself.

Weak Lips

Playing the trumpet is to your lips what lifting weights are to your muscles. To play the trumpet, you have to press your lips together and make a buzzing sound. When your press your lips together to the business end of a trumpet, the buzzing comes out the party end as a tone. The more you play, the stronger your lips get. But before they get strong, they get weak.

By day three of camp, all of the trumpet players' lips were weak. We had packed at least thirty hours of playing into the week thus far. The mouthpiece pressing your lips against your teeth rubs the insides of your lips raw. Not only does it hurt, you can't play anymore. Your lips just won't buzz.

Enter Anbesol, a brand of over-the-counter dental pain medication. Trumpet players use it to get themselves through band camp. Rub a little of that magic on your lips and they get nice and tingly and numb . . . at least enough so you can play again. It is also worth knowing that Anbesol comes in two forms: gel and liquid. And therein lies the necessary quotient to our equation, one that has given me countless laughs through the years.

Unexpected Results

I don't remember who came up with the idea or how they did so. But somewhere along the line, Arthur was dared to drink the bottle of liquid Anbesol he had brought with him to camp. And I'm not sure why, but he said yes and swallowed it down without much thought. At first Arthur felt nothing but the thrill of victory. Not only had he proven himself worthy among his comrades, he also had a funny, tingly feeling inside him that made him giggle like a school girl. Though the thrill of victory would soon be replaced with the agony of defeat—dinner. If I remember correctly, the entree of choice at the cafeteria that week was grilled cheese.

Now I don't want to go into too much detail here, so let's just say that whatever it is in Anbesol that numbs your lips evidently also numbs your digestive tract. Arthur gave new meaning to the band's motivational saying: "Leave a little of yourself on the field."

Positive Peer Pressure

I know this story is gross, but it does have a point. Peer pressure is a lot like that little bottle of Anbesol. It has the potential to be powerfully destructive in our lives. Peer pressure can push us to make the wrong choices, even when the right choice is in front of us. And I could continue to flesh out this analogy, but I'm not telling you anything you don't already know and haven't already heard a hundred other times. You don't need to hear it again.

What you may not realize, though, is that peer pressure equally has the potential to be powerfully positive. If used correctly, the Anbesol could have been healing and relieving to Arthur. We are the same way. We have that same great potential.

Our Opportunities

Every day we have the opportunity to have positive influences on dozens of people. Do you take advantage of them? Are you the person who says thank you with a smile to the restaurant server? Or are you the person who flashes a dirty look and makes a snide comment when the server makes a mistake on the order? Next time you're at a restaurant, try the smile. Notice what impact it has on the server and how you are treated for the rest of the meal. More interestingly, notice what impact it has on the other people at your table. Chances are they will end up following your lead, dishing out their own kindness without even noticing it.

Every day we have the opportunity to have positive influences on dozens of people.

Those are the opportunities I'm talking about. Dozens of little moments each day that could be spent loving other people. Because really, that's what being a source of positive peer pressure is all about—loving people.

And there is no better example of that than a man named Jesus. He hasn't walked the earth in two thousand years, yet we still hear stories of his kindness. How he affected the lives of his friends. How he affected the lives of people who had never met him. His kindness and love left a legacy. That's a legacy I wouldn't mind leaving either.

Happy Friday

On Friday something good happened to me. My hatefulness went away. I realized that no one is perfect. The reason I hated everyone is because I have been lonely for a long time. I hated myself, but I can't help the way I look, and nothing can change it. One day God will give me a girlfriend. Thank you, God, that the war in me has ended.

by Robbie Fletcher (written at age 16)

by Emily Downs

A COFFEEHOUSE WITNESS

I had never shared so close a space with anyone who looked like him.

We need to take advantage of every opportunity to share the good news of Christ Jesus. I firmly believe the Word of God and the truth of the gospel message and know, without doubt, that accepting Jesus Christ as Lord and Savior is the only way to life everlasting. Yet as much as I know this to be true, I find myself afraid to share this saving news with those around me.

I feel like I am too young, too inexperienced, or just too shy. I become easily flustered when the subject of God comes up around non-Christians, who appear to have all the answers for not believing in Jesus. It seems every time I watch a movie or read a modern book, the teenagers hate church or mock God. I am afraid that if I speak about being a Christian, my peers will immediately categorize me as uncool or a religious freak who would never do anything fun. So, most of the time, I bite my tongue and just listen with guilt as they mock my Lord. I'm ashamed of my many lost opportunities to share Christ with lost people.

Strange-looking Stranger

One day I was hanging out in a coffee shop doing homework and my daily devotions, which involve reading a few chapters of the Bible. The shop was particularly busy that day, and a guy asked if he could share my table. I agreed and thought nothing of it until he took the chair across from mine.

Looking up, I was surprised to see a very gothic-looking guy—with dyed long black hair, too many piercings to count, and, to my horror, a shirt printed with satanic symbols! I had never shared so close a space with anyone who looked like him. I felt uneasy. Here I was reading the Bible; he probably hated Christians. I kept my head down, trying to concentrate on the words, but my mind kept wandering back to my strange tablemate.

Much to my despair, he spoke to me.

"You're reading the Bible," he said.

Oh no, I thought. *Is he going to start cursing God or saying horrible things about Christians?*

I looked up and forced a smile, "Yes, I read it almost every day." Why had I said that? I didn't want to evoke a conversation with this dark stranger!

"So, you're a Christian?" he asked.

"Yes," I answered, still smiling. I didn't want him to know I was intimidated.

"I've studied different religions," he informed me.

"Well, I am not religious," I reported. "I just believe in Jesus Christ as my Savior." Where did that come from? Why did I need to share my beliefs with this stranger?

"You believe there is only one true religion?"

Oh, Lord, I thought. *I am so bad at this! What do I say? My words always come out wrong.* I pleaded to God to give me the right thing to say.

"Yes," I answered, "but I wouldn't use the word *religion*. I believe there is only one way to God and heaven, which is through his Son, Jesus Christ."

"I don't believe in heaven like that. I think it's different for everyone."

"I think there is only one heaven and only one way to get there."

The Answers I Needed

I wondered if he could hear the trembling in my voice, for I couldn't believe I was having this conversation. As we talked I kept a silent prayer going in my head. I felt like I didn't know what to say, but I kept coming up with answers. I studied the guy and was surprised to find he had a nice face and it was actually easy to talk with him.

> *Though I felt unprepared and even nervous about sharing my faith, God gave me the answers I needed.*

The guy told me he thought all religions were right. I disagreed, saying there was only one God and one way to him—through Jesus Christ. Though I felt unprepared and even nervous about sharing my faith with a complete stranger, God gave me the answers I needed when I needed them. Jesus was with me the whole time! I didn't have great answers, but I gave correct ones, and I feel certain the Lord was able to use me in spite of my youth and fear.

I may never know what happened with the guy in the coffee shop, but I am certain the Lord equipped me to be his ambassador that day. God often uses many people to reach one person. We are all to be laborers in the field God has prepared—some may plant, others may water—but the Lord will bring in the harvest. Often we do not see the end result of our labor, but we can trust that God has a plan. Our job is simply to obey his command to tell the world about Jesus Christ.

You never know when you will have an opportunity to share the Lord with someone. If you are listening to the Holy Spirit's prompting, you too will be ready for such an encounter.

by Jennifer Dunning

SITTING IN SILENCE

I dared not speak a word as I sat and watched the events unfold.

I sat there in disbelief feeling the sweat in the palms of my hands. *Someone should say something*, I thought to myself. But I dared not speak a word as I sat and watched the events unfold.

Sunday Morning Mischief

Several students had arrived early for Sunday school, and we found ourselves waiting patiently for our teacher. The minutes ticked by as we filled each other in on the week's activities. It appeared to be a typical Sunday morning. But the mood changed rather suddenly when two of the young men who were leaders in our group made their way into the kitchen of the small house in which we met.

Inside the kitchen were several bags of wrapped Christmas presents that had been collected by the congregation to be delivered to needy children. The guys returned quickly, smiling proudly as they each began to tear open numerous toy motorcycles that were intended for the less fortunate.

The lump in my throat was now competing with the knot in my stomach as I watched this display of selfishness and insubordination. At any minute, the teacher would arrive. But before she did, the two realized they should attempt to cover the tracks of their mischievous deeds. The trash was collected and crammed into a small metal garbage can the guys had placed in the middle of the room.

With a smug grin, one of the young men retrieved a pack of matches from his coat pocket. Countless things flashed through my mind as I stared in disbelief. But still I sat in silence.

With nothing more than one quick stroke of a match, flames began to dance high above the rim of the garbage can. For a moment, it looked as if their actions would go unnoticed until, at this moment, our teacher made her grand entrance. After a few shrieks of astonishment, she quickly tossed the can out into the snow. Her next words were ones I will never forget.

She looked at each of us and said, "I am disappointed in you. I asked these guys to do this today to test you and see which of you would stand up for what is right and speak the truth."

It was a test I failed miserably.

Deborah's Bold Leadership

I thought about that smoky Sunday school class as I read the story of Deborah (Judges 4). I had not seen myself as qualified to speak out and be a leader among my peers. For Deborah, living in a time when women were not typically the voice of leadership, was it easy for her to speak up?

Scripture tells us Deborah was a judge and a prophetess. Being a judge, she was gifted with wisdom and settled many disputes among the Israelites. Being a prophetess, her wisdom and the truth she spoke were given to her by God. But in a time when women were seen and not heard, was it easy those first few times she spoke God's words out loud? Surely there were people who mocked her and doubted that her gifts were genuine. Many must have scoffed and tried to silence her.

Knowing God's truth is the easy part. Living it is a bit harder.

The book of Judges shows us a repeating cycle for the Israelites. They would be lured away from God time and again by the appealing nature of pagan gods. Time and again, they found themselves oppressed by evil rulers as punishment for their idolatry. And time and again, God would send a judge to speak his truth and establish peace again. He sent Deborah with a message for his people, which she was not afraid to share.

Message of Truth

Today, regardless of our gender, we face the same test I believe Deborah faced daily. We are surrounded by opportunities to speak God's truth, and yet we are often silenced by the fear that someone will ridicule us. We look the other way and pretend we do not see the countless sins that surround us each day. We remain silent.

God sends us today with a message for his people. Our job is no different than Deborah's. Knowing God's truth is the easy part. Living it is harder. Speaking God's Word boldly is where many of us get tripped up.

Deborah was an amazing but unlikely leader. And if you think you are unqualified, you may be silently watching others floundering in sin. Speak God's truth boldly regardless of the price.

My teacher's words of disappointment that day still ring in my ears. I will speak up now and avoid hearing that same disappointment in the voice of my heavenly father.

by Jay Arrington

REMEMBERING MY GRANDFATHER

It may sound strange, but I miss him even though I never knew him.

I don't really remember my grandfather because he died several months before my second birthday. The vision I have of him comes from pictures and videos I've seen. You may wonder how someone I didn't know could have an impact on my life. There are several ways.

Family Name

My grandfather's name was Asbury Neely. When I was born, my parents named me James Asbury, although I go by Jay. (James is for my father and his father.) Asbury is an unusual name. Some people say it is strange, but I think it is cool. I don't know anyone else with that name, although there is an Asbury Park in New Jersey and an Asbury College in Kentucky. (Nice of them to name a college after me!)

My grandfather's name was important to him because it was a family name, and he loved his family a lot. He was one of nine children. The verse in Proverbs about a good name being better than great riches is one I think about when I remember my grandfather—with nine children they certainly weren't rich.

Good Looks and Good Humor

Everyone tells me I'm like my grandfather. Physically, my body build is like his—tall and thin. My mom has pictures of my grandfather at my age, and we look alike. Ladies who knew him say he was really good-looking.

People say we're alike in other ways too. He had a great sense of humor and was famous for telling jokes. I like to make people laugh, but instead of telling jokes I do funny voices and accents.

Hobbies

My grandfather was a building contractor. There are houses and buildings all over town that he built. I enjoy building things also. The difference is I build skateboard ramps. I like working with lumber, and I guess he did too.

When my grandfather died, my grandmother kept his 1977 Chevrolet station wagon. It is still sitting in her garage even though it doesn't run now. My dad and I are working on getting it running again so I can drive it when I get my license next year. It will be cool to ride around town and haul lumber in the same car my grandfather drove.

Spiritual Growth

If I had to choose one way I most want to be like my grandfather when I grow up it would be spiritually. My grandfather was active in his church, the same church

I am a member of now. I know from stories my mom has told me that my grandfather knew the importance of prayer and Bible study. I'm learning and growing in my faith through my youth discipleship group. I think my grandfather would be glad I'm doing that.

I really wish my grandfather had lived longer because it would have been nice to grow up with him around. I'm sure we would have done a lot of things together. It may sound strange, but I miss him even though I never knew him. I don't really want to think about it right now, but one day I'll get to spend time with him in heaven.

My grandfather has influenced my life in big and small ways, and I'm thankful. If your grandfather is still alive, go spend some time with him. There's a lot you can learn.

WHAT'S THE POINT?

> "I am worn out calling for help; my throat is parched. My eyes fail, looking for my God."
>
> —Psalm 69:3

by Sarah Ooms

FIGHTING FOR HOPE

I was begging God to kill me and wishing I had the guts to end my life myself.

The end of my ninth-grade year was the worst time of my life. Yet it also taught me the most. For those eight months I was fighting—fighting myself, my friends, my family, even God.

Looking for Answers

I was looking for answers to those tough questions that we all ask sometime during our lives. I pulled away from the people who loved me the most to spend time just being alone. I hated myself the whole time, but I was still the only person I wanted to be with. Finally I couldn't stand myself either. Then I started to figure out more who I was—the real me. But the more I got to know myself, the clearer it became how pathetic I really was. I could see who I wanted to be, but the distance between that person and who I was right then was just too deep.

Somehow during all this I did manage to grow closer to God. He was the one I felt I could really talk to. Still I chose to ignore everything he was trying to tell me about my true worth. I wanted more than anything to change who I was. I wanted to be on fire for God and be doing great things for him. But instead I was sitting in my room at war with myself.

Finally I decided that there were some things I could have control over. I became obsessed with calories, skipping meals, and making myself throw up. My friends noticed some of the time, but I blew them off and made excuses. I saw my life turn into one big lie. I felt like I was a total fake no matter who I was with, and I couldn't even be honest with myself.

Begging to Die

Every night I would sit alone in the dark and cry. I knew I had all the symptoms of depression, but I wasn't willing to get help from the right people. Finally it got to the point where every time I got in the car, I was hoping it would crash. Each night my last thought before I fell asleep was that maybe somehow I would never wake up. I was begging God to kill me and wishing I had the guts to end my life myself.

Thoughts of death and suicide were constantly in the back of my mind. I wrote letters to my friends for them to read after I died. Life was spinning out of control, but I didn't even care. At first it had scared me, but then I got to the point where I didn't feel anything but a chilling numbness inside that froze my heart.

I started to doubt everything I had ever known to be true. I convinced myself that I had sold my soul to the devil and I was going to hell. But I figured that even that didn't matter, because eternity in hell couldn't be all that much worse than this fake life I was living.

If the main point of hell was separation from God, I felt that was no different than how my life was already.

Eventually more of my friends found out what was going on, and their prayers and encouragement helped—for a while. But Satan was attacking as much as ever. Some nights I could feel a dark and evil presence in my room that would not leave. I believe that demons were there a lot of times, but I didn't know how to fight them, and I didn't even care enough to try. I clung to my pain instead of the truth, and I let it control me. I didn't want to get better and have to deal with life.

Planning on Suicide

July 23, 2003, was a day I will never forget. All the problems in my mind seemed to reach their climax that night. My friends were frustrated with my depression, no one understood me, I felt totally useless, and I wasn't sure if I still even believed in God. Life was no longer worth living. As I sat through youth group that night, I was making plans to commit suicide. I had thought about it many times before, but that night I had a specific plan and I wasn't afraid. I remember driving home that night, thinking that I would never pass that way again.

Somehow I didn't get to carry out my plans. God must have told both my youth minister and his wife that I was desperate that night. All I had told them was that I felt like a hypocrite and didn't want to sing with the band. They both mentioned to my mom that I was having a really bad day. So when I got home, my parents sat me down and made me talk to them for a while. I wasn't totally honest with them and didn't tell them just how bad a day it was. I still planned on ending my life once they were done.

But then they finally let me go to bed, and my mom said she would come in and check on me later. By then I figured my plans for that night were ruined, and I was feeling a little better. I went to sleep that night assuming that another bad night would come when I would carry out my plans.

I found out a few days later that two of my closest friends couldn't sleep that night and had stayed up and prayed for me.

Finding a Purpose

The next day my parents convinced me to go see a doctor. I was diagnosed with depression. I got medication that helped me a lot, and I figured that would be the end to my problems.

But my best friend cared enough about me to ask me some tough questions. She asked how I could expect some pills to take away all my problems for the rest of my life. That really forced me to think about my priorities and what I really believed.

> *I've found a purpose for life that goes beyond my temporary feelings and trials.*

Not long after that I rededicated my life to Christ. It isn't always easy, and there are still some dark times, but I've found a purpose for life that goes beyond my temporary feelings and trials. I know my life today is a miracle, and I don't take anything for granted anymore. I believe now that there was a reason I went through that pain—God really used it to make me a better person.

Romans 5:2-5 says, "We rejoice in the hope of the glory of God. Not only so, but we also rejoice in our sufferings, because we know that suffering produces perseverance; perseverance, character; and character, hope. And hope does not disappoint us."

Never Alone

Will I always be alone?
Sometimes I sit in complete solitude
  wondering
Is it worth it?
The masquerade I've been sucked into
Although, it's nothing but shadows
  Hiding the true me
  the way I think
  the way I feel
All shut out by what the world thinks
  could be
And not what should be
Only being heard by your ears
I'm screaming at the top of my lungs
Can you help me?
I stop in complete solitude knowing
  I'm never alone

by Victoria Linson (written at age 14)

by Jessica Paugh

NO VALLEY LOW ENOUGH

I actually had something to drive now, all because of my friend.

Tears filled my eyes. "It's mine?" I asked hesitantly.

Shannon grinned, but her own watery eyes gave her away.

"It's all yours," she said. "You have been such a blessing in my life, I wanted to bless you back." Then she threw her arms around me.

As I returned Shannon's hug, I clenched the slender car key in my hand. The image of the gold Mercury Sable, its deep red interior still cluttered with Shannon's things, filled my mind. I actually had something to drive, all because of the friend I was now sharing a warm hug with.

She suddenly giggled. I pulled back to see her eyes shining—and not just because of the tears.

"This is a better reaction than I expected!" Shannon said.

If she only knew why.

Loneliness

I was lonely. Not because no one loved me—I had a wonderful family and great friends—but because I couldn't feel God. On the breezy mountaintop of my spiritual walk, I have felt his presence as close as the person standing next to me. Then there are the valleys, when it seems like God has stepped completely out of my life.

I had been in a valley for months.

It seemed like I had always been there and always would be. Would I ever stop getting mere glimpses of those high mountains and actually get out of the valley?

During this time, my family and friends, especially Shannon, were great sources of comfort. Shannon and I worked together in the preschool class at church, and every Sunday morning she made it a point to give me a big hug and ask how my week had been. We had been friends for a long time, and her sensitivity to the needs of others was a tremendous blessing.

Never Leaving

Shannon soon found out I was looking for a car. "I prayed and prayed," she told me later, "and I couldn't get away from the fact that God wanted you to have my old car."

God himself had picked out this car for me? The Lord of the universe saw me in my little valley and reached for me with a gentle hand, saying, "Here I am. I have never left you, and I never will." He used Shannon's gift to show me that he will never forget me or leave me, even in those dark, cold valleys.

Every morning after that, when I walked outside to see my car parked in the driveway, I was again reminded that, although the world might overlook me,

God never will. No matter how low the valley gets, he will always be here.

by Ronica Stromberg

AT THE POINT OF PAIN

Within minutes, neon, squiggly lines floated before my eyes. I tried to keep standing but passed out.

That July when I turned fifteen, I had it all—a part-time job, great friends, and a schedule designed to squeeze in every ounce of fun from a summer vacation already half gone.

Unknown to me, I also had an illness to be loathed.

The first sign of it came only days after my birthday. I was standing in the kitchen that morning, hurriedly stacking my breakfast dishes in the dishwasher, when my eyesight blurred. I blinked, but the blurriness remained. Within minutes, neon, squiggly lines floated before my eyes. Soon my eyesight failed completely, leaving me staring into nothing. No color. Nothing. I tried to keep standing but passed out.

When I came to, I lay shivering on the linoleum floor. I stumbled to my bedroom and, despite the sweltering July heat, wrapped myself in a quilt. I alternated between hot and cold flashes, between casting off the quilt and pulling it back on.

My stomach churned, my head spun, and I began vomiting. Unlike with a flu bug, the vomiting brought no relief from the hot-and-cold churning illness that had overtaken me.

What is this? I agonized. *I'm too young for a serious illness, aren't I?* I spent the day in fearful prayer, waiting for the misery to pass.

Treatable, but Not Curable

The misery did pass, but in a few months it returned again. A few months after that, it came again.

My mother grew concerned. "You turn absolutely gray when this happens," she said. "I've never seen anyone look so ill." She avoided saying words such as "brain tumor," but the fear in her eyes told me what she was thinking.

"Maybe we should visit a doctor," she said.

We visited several. After the doctors performed a CAT scan and numerous tests, they arrived at the same conclusion: I suffered from migraine headaches.

Migraine headaches? What? All this over a headache? It seemed impossible.

The doctors assured me, though, that it was very possible. Even though the majority of people who suffer from migraines do not experience symptoms as strong as mine, there are some who do, the doctors said. The causes, they said, are often unknown. Although migraines are treatable, they are seldom curable. The doctors offered medication but cautioned me on the side effects.

I decided against taking the medication because of my age and fear of the effects of long-term drug use. I prayed for relief from this condition instead.

Months passed without incident, but the migraines returned—again and again. I puzzled over why God would allow me to be afflicted with such an illness and wondered how I should deal with it.

A Thorn in My Flesh

I found answers in the Bible when I learned that the apostle Paul also suffered from an illness he despised. He referred to it as "a thorn in my flesh, a messenger of Satan, to torment me" (2 Corinthians 12:7). The strength of his words is shown when one remembers he has already suffered through being flogged, lashed, beaten with rods, stoned, and shipwrecked!

> *I learned that the apostle Paul too suffered from an illness he despised.*

What illness did Paul suffer from? Over the years, theologians have offered various possibilities, most based on this passage of Scripture in 2 Corinthians and the passage dealing with Paul's conversion (Acts 9:1-19). They point out that, before his conversion, Paul (then known as Saul) fell to the ground after a light from heaven flashed around him. He was blinded for three days after that, and he regained his sight after something like scales fell from his eyes. They suggest Paul might have suffered from epileptic seizures, an eye disease, or even migraines!

Whatever Paul's "thorn" might have been, the approach he took to dealing with it is plain. First, he asked God to take it away (2 Corinthians 12:8). Then, when God chose not to, Paul came to accept it—even to boast of it (verse 9). He recognized that the weakness kept him from becoming conceited, and it allowed God's power to be shown in his life.

"That is why," he wrote, "for Christ's sake, I delight in weaknesses, in insults, in hardships, in persecutions, in difficulties. For when I am weak, then I am strong" (verse 10).

Paul's words give me direction for living with illness. Through his life and that of other people around me, I see I have the choice to be consumed by illness or to find a way to conquer through it. I realize I am not alone in my suffering and my suffering is not without purpose. When I am laid low, God stands tall. I draw comfort from the knowledge that my life is in his hands—hands already pierced out of love for me.

by Jeanne Zornes

BEST OF TIMES, WORST OF TIMES

I'd always been a good student. Now I wondered if I'd fail my first class.

Finals week had come—and as I slid into my front-row seat for my English exam, I thought of the opening of the Charles Dickens novel *A Tale of Two Cities:* "It was the best of times, it was the worst of times."

For me, "the best of times" was getting closer to college graduation. But "the worst of times" was this class. I took a big breath as I gripped the small blue-covered exam book every student had to buy at the campus bookstore for essay tests.

I just wanted to get through this test, one of three I faced that day. Worse, I'd come down with a bug. My head hurt and my stomach churned, but I was determined to get through the day. I'd worked so hard to pass this class.

The professor strode in and handed out our essay questions, and immediately I felt even more sick. None of the questions asked what I'd studied.

Boring!

I'd always been a good student, graduating from high school with a 3.9 GPA. In college I got mostly A's and B's. Now I wondered if I'd fail my first class. I couldn't. I had one more quarter until graduation and couldn't fit in a repeat.

I hadn't wanted to take this particular class on Victorian literature. Others had warned me about it: "Don't take a class from *that* teacher." But I needed one more English literature class, and nothing else fit into my schedule.

The teacher looked Victorian—wan with thin, gray hair and a grumpy face, like a Scrooge transplanted to the next century. I listened to lectures as bland as library paste. The books were tedious. Some nights I'd fall asleep trying to navigate hundred-year-old sentences that ran on for half a page.

Yet I gave the class my best effort. Besides sitting in front to stay attentive, I kept up on readings and took detailed notes to prep for the professor's quizzes. I met with him once to strategize my big research paper, but his coldness made me feel like I was wasting his time. I asked God to get me past the negatives and help me focus for the ten weeks of the class.

Now, as I stared at the exam, I wondered if all that was for nothing. Somehow, over the next hour, I filled the exam book with "blah" fluff. As we dismissed, the teacher said we could get our finals back next term in his office.

More Than I Deserved

Home for spring break, I moped all week, dreading what my parents would say about my flunked class. Grades were mailed to our homes.

"Mail for you," Mom called that Friday. My fingers shaking, I slit open the official envelope and scanned the grades. I saw the expected A's and B's, then my eyes locked on the grade for Victorian lit: Not a D or an F as I had expected. I got a B!

Mercy, pure mercy. I had never expected that from a Scrooge look-alike.

The next week, as classes resumed, I headed for my teacher's office. The hallway squeaked under my feet as I considered what to say.

"I'm here for my exam book," I said when he opened the door. In that awkward silence as he ruffled through a stack, I knew I had to ask.

"I was happy but surprised to get a B in your class," I began. "I was sick and wrote a poor final."

"I know," he agreed. "Your final didn't represent your other work during the term. I chose to ignore the final."

Mercy, pure mercy. I had never expected that from a Scrooge look-alike.

Two Lessons

I learned two lessons that day. One was to be careful about rumored reputations, even about professors. How often had I judged people on externals? I knew that was wrong: "Man looks at the outward appearance, but the Lord look at the heart" (1 Samuel 16:7).

The other was a fresh vision of God's mercy. I didn't deserve that B, but I got it because the teacher overlooked my failures on the final. But if God had been the teacher, and the class was life, his mercy would have given me an A+ in spite of failing the final and all assignments.

It goes back to what Romans 3:21-26 says—that everybody falls short of God's standard. But God wiped out those sins by sending Jesus to die for them in my place. I like how the prophet Jeremiah put it: "The unfailing love of the Lord never ends! By his mercies we have been kept from complete destruction. Great is his faithfulness; his mercies begin afresh each day" (Lamentations 3:22, 23, *NLT*).

Yes, that class was the worst of times but also the best of times—because God used an exam book to write another story about grace.

by April Stier

SOLID ROCK

Everything I held dear to me had been shattered by life's wrecking ball, and my world lay in ruins.

"Dear Jesus."

The words escaped my lips before wrenching sobs overtook my body. I laid my arms on the chair in front of me and quickly buried my face to muffle the sound of my pain. The walls of the chapel at the hospital echoed my cries. A large cross and a few rows of chairs were my only companions. The clock had struck midnight hours ago, but my family refused to leave Mom's side while she fought for her life in intensive care. I had stayed strong for my family all day, but I couldn't hold back my emotions any longer.

I had nothing left. Everything I held dear had been shattered by life's wrecking ball, and my world lay in ruins. I didn't know how many more of life's hard knocks I could take.

Rattled Foundations

My foundation first began to rattle during Christmas break. Dad called a family meeting, and that only meant one thing: something was wrong, and we needed to discuss and work it out. Characteristic of Dad's forthright personality, his next words didn't soften the truth.

"We have no more money. You and Christopher will have to find a way to pay for your education by yourselves next year or you won't be able to return to college."

The news hit me like a blast of dynamite. Pay for college myself? I couldn't come up with that kind of money in such a short time! I already had a job, but everything I was bringing in there was paying off my second semester. Even if I worked all summer, I could never come up with enough to pay for an entire year of school.

I felt my stomach tighten into a ball of tension. I knew we were having financial problems, but I had never guessed things were this bad. The possibility of taking time off from school terrified me. I had dreamed of college since I was ten years old. I loved everything about my new life—the independence, my classes, the campus, my friends. The thought of postponing my dream and moving home to work a full-time job caused tears to prick my eyes.

I was scared, but I wasn't going to let fear overrule my reason. I knew that if God wanted me to remain in school, he would provide a way. My foundations were shaken, but my trust in God did not collapse. God would place me where I needed to be.

Completely Shattered

The next whack of the wrecking ball hit in January. I came home for a weekend to visit my great-grandmother, who was dying, but a phone call late Friday night knocked me to my knees. My brother's college roommate, Jake, had been in a serious car accident. Jake died Saturday afternoon, just before I arrived at the hospital with my parents. We had been neighbors for years, and my brother and I grew up playing with Jake and his brother and sisters. His death devastated my entire family.

The anguish of possibly losing Mom was more than I could bear.

Two months later, I found myself at the hospital again. The day of Jake's funeral Mom ran a fever. A week later she caught a cold. As each week passed, her cold progressively worsened until she landed in the hospital in March with pneumonia. The doctors treated her, but she still did not improve. They ran some more tests and diagnosed her with congestive heart failure. The virus she had been battling for a month had settled in her heart, which now functioned at less than 15 percent capacity.

The doctors said the only thing keeping her alive was her will to live. The wrecking ball hit its final mark, and my world completely shattered.

Clinging Desperately

Alone in the hospital chapel, words could not express my pain as the broken pieces of my life settled around me. I couldn't imagine life without Mom, and the anguish of possibly losing her was more than I could bear. I had been through so much during the past few months. When was this devastation going to end?

But even as I lay hurting and bleeding before my creator, I felt him wipe away my tears. He eased my terror and replaced it with his peace. Suddenly, I knew everything was going to be all right. I didn't know what the future held, but I felt God's strength lift me out of life's ruins. I desperately clung to Jesus and promised to trust him no matter what happened.

Mom was released from the hospital two weeks later, but she was an invalid. I moved home from college in May only to find our circumstances even more dire. Our already tight finances had completely diminished. We were only a few hundred dollars from bankruptcy. As Dad and I sorted through bills we couldn't pay, we told each other God would provide. He had seen us through this far; he wouldn't abandon us now.

Healing Summer

During the summer months, I experienced God's faithfulness in a whole new way. People brought us meals three or four times a week so we didn't have to buy groceries. Women from the church cleaned our house every week for free, and men from the church mowed our lawn. We managed to pay all our bills, and by God's grace, I won several scholarships. Both my brother and I returned to college in the fall, each with a full ride.

> *He had seen us through this far; he wouldn't abandon us now.*

God had filled our lives with abundant blessings, but his greatest blessing came at the end of June. Mom felt led by the Holy Spirit to be anointed with oil—according to James 5:14—so one Sunday we gathered in our minister's office and laid hands on her and prayed for her healing.

Since that day, her health has progressively improved. Before, walking from her bedroom to the living room wiped her out. Now she can walk around all day without fatigue. Though the doctors didn't think she would ever function normally again, Mom is almost completely healed. She is a miracle!

Tough times are never fun, but they are powerful teaching lessons. My faith in God has grown strong and steady. When life stripped me of everything, God never left my side. He was all I had left, and even though everything else was crashing around me, he never moved. He gave me strength when I had none; he gave me peace in my darkest moments.

When life knocked me down, Jesus Christ picked me up. He proved to me life's wrecking ball would never be able to crack or crumble his faithfulness to me. He is the solid rock.

My World of Tears

Welcome to my world of tears,
A place of my stored pains and fears.
I will not often open this door
Know you walk on hallowed floor.
Most just see the pasted smiles
I keep within my many files
Of masks I use to hide behind
So my real face stays only mine.
You may see different walls
Quite a lot fills these halls,
Memories both new and old
A collected part of this great fold.
Scenes or emotions fill these spaces
From many different times and places.
You'd be surprised how far they go;
I was young when it began to grow
Into a large but hidden closet,
Where my secret wounds I could deposit.
So few have even seen this land
I could yet count them on my hand.
So if you really want to see
The real and true uncovered me
Then open both your eyes and ears
And welcome to my world of tears.

by Lindsay Anderson (written at age 17)

GOD'S BIG DREAMS

I began hiding my learning disabilities from my friends.

When I was in elementary school, I was diagnosed with dyslexia. At first I thought it was kind of cool that I got to go to special classes. My mom didn't really explain to me that I'd been labeled "dyslexic," so I didn't understand the reasons behind everything.

Hiding My Weaknesses

In middle school, I really began to realize what the special classes were all about. I understood I was part of the group because I wasn't keeping up. I began hiding my learning disabilities from my friends. They would ask for my schedule so we could see if we had classes together. I would always figure out a way to change the subject; I became a master at this.

Little things to other people were big things to me. Like fire drills—those were huge because you had to walk out in line with your classmates. I'd always get lost in the crowd and try to hide because I thought if anyone finds out I'm in these learning disability classes, they're going to think I'm dumb or they're not going to want to be my friend anymore. I grew into a young adult who felt that God probably thought I was dumb too. *Well, I guess God can use other people, but what's he ever going to do with me?* I felt pretty small for years.

Avoiding My Abilities

After high school, I attended The Baptist College of Florida as a music major. There were other things I wanted to do, but I thought I'd be safer as a music major, especially when I considered my learning disabilities.

I really had little hope of God using me at all. I just didn't feel "good enough" before him.

One day, an English professor came up to me and asked, "You're dyslexic, aren't you?" I immediately said no. He said, "You're drawing pictures with words here. You have a knack for this; you need to do it more." I'd never heard anyone say that. I always stayed as far away from the written word as I could, for obvious reasons.

Later in college a guy walked up to me and asked, "Hey, you want to be a youth pastor?" I said, "No way, man." I was about twenty-one, and I thought, *I've got a fiery temper, I don't know what to say, I'm dyslexic, and I have ADD.* I never wanted to do anything where I had to teach in front of people anyway. I just thought I didn't have the talents or skills that would lead anywhere near that goal. I let my insecurities and my labels hold me back from exploring the options God had in store.

Living My Passions

I stayed a music major, but since I was at a Bible college I also studied missions, evangelism, Old Testament, New Testament, all those classes. You get all the Bible and ministry classes with any degree. Eventually, after a long, hard struggle with myself, I realized youth ministry really was where my passion flamed. I decided not to let my fears hold me back.

> *I decided not to let my fears hold me back.*

I ended up being hired to work with youth at a church, and we started a teen worship band called Casting Crowns. We made CDs for our youth group to give away at school. When you opened one up, you'd read it and it would say, "This is Refuge, one of our youth programs, we do this on Wednesday nights; we have Bible Study Fellowship on Sunday morning," and so on.

A student named Chase took the CD to basketball camp with him. Mark Miller of the country music group Sawyer Brown happened to know one of the coaches there and was at the camp visiting. Chase bumped into Mark, and they started talking. When Chase found out Mark was a believer he was like, "Hey man, you have to hear my youth pastor's CD."

Sharing My Story

That's how all this happened. We didn't have demos going out. It wasn't something that we saw coming. Casting Crowns was just a youth group band. When God brought it to be, it didn't suddenly nullify everything else we were doing. We decided in the middle of it, *God if you want us to do both, we're doing both.* It just grew from there.

I didn't think God could use people who were a little less than others.

The song "Voice of Truth," from our first record, talks a lot about my experiences with dyslexia and not feeling good enough. I get tons of letters because of my testimony. I talk a lot in concert about the dyslexia and ADD thing and how the fear kept me quiet. It boiled down to the fact that I was scared to try and do this thing I thought God wanted me to do. I thought God needed the best of the best. I didn't think he could use people who were a little less than others.

Eventually, I started seeing in 2 Corinthians 12 that Paul had issues too. He had thorns in his flesh, and he got down about it. God told him, My grace is sufficient for you, my power is made perfect in your weakness. That message has really rung true with so many people I've met on the road and in e-mails. That's been big.

I almost missed student ministry because I didn't think I'd be any good at it. Now when I talk to my teenagers at church, I tell them about my experiences. I say, "You're deciding what you're going to do in the future based on what you might be good at today. That's dangerous. God's got a dream for your life, and it's bigger than yours."

by Charity Thomas

DISCOVERING I WAS BIPOLAR

I was in a mental hospital. How had this happened? What was the matter with me?

With trembling fingers, I punched into my phone the number of my friend, Kathi.

"You'll never believe what I just did," I told her when she answered. "I can't believe it."

"What did you do?" she asked casually. It was nothing unusual for me to call at 11:30 on a Thursday night.

"I swallowed a whole bottle of ibuprofen." I stared at the empty container in my hand.

"Why don't you come over here?" Kathi invited. Her voice still sounded relaxed. Only later would I learn how frightened she was.

"OK." I was in PJs, but it was a warm May night and her apartment was only two buildings away. I started walking, not noticing I didn't have my glasses or shoes.

"We're going to the hospital," Kathi told me when I arrived. Her roommate, Beth, nodded vigorously.

I stared at them. "Why? I don't need to."

Kathi grabbed her car keys. "Come on, Charity."

I started to protest. "This is all just a foolish mistake! I've taken ibuprofen before . . ."

Kathi took one of my arms and Beth the other. Before I knew it, I was in the emergency room. The next few hours were a blur—an IV inserted in my hand, a tube down my throat, my stomach pumped, charcoal all over my pajamas, blood work, an X-ray.

By 8 AM I was being hustled into a van for transport to the Behavioral Health Center. That's right—I was taken to a mental hospital. How had this happened? Why had I taken a drug overdose? What was the matter with me?

Tough Semester, Tough Year

I was a senior in college, and it was the last week of classes. The next Monday was final exams, and then graduation!

I was ready—it had been a tough year. I'd dealt with roommate problems, a miserable but required class called Senior Seminar, and an impossibly hard philosophy course I'd recently dropped. Though that meant I was short a few credits for my degree, the college was letting me go through the ceremony. I was already signed up to take philosophy in June at another school near home.

With all that, plus job-hunting, I was struggling. I'd prayed, seen a counselor, and taken anti-depressant medication. Nothing seemed to help much. But I'd finished most of my coursework and had only a few exams to take. After several days of the flu, I was feeling better physically.

That evening I'd gone to a friend's to watch a favorite TV show. But when I'd returned, my headache was back and I felt feverish. I remembered opening a new bottle of painkillers, but that was all. The next thing I knew, I was dialing Kathi and holding the empty container.

Diagnosis

When we arrived at the mental hospital, I only wanted to sleep. Exhausted from being up all night, my throat raw from the tube that pumped my stomach, my hand throbbing from the poorly inserted IV, I staggered into my room.

After lunch that day, I met with the psychiatrist. She had my file from my school counselor.

"Charity, I think you have bipolar disorder," she said.

I had no idea what that was. Unknown to me, my counselor had suspected this might be my problem.

The doctor explained it used to be called manic depression. Many of the symptoms she described were familiar. Racing thoughts and not being able to keep my mind on what I wanted it to think about. Deep depression, followed by a high where I just had to do something, anything.

She felt I had the less-severe type two. People with this disease type usually responded well to the medication she was having me start.

How had I become bipolar? It's thought to have a genetic link, although no one I knew of in my family had it. That's not unusual since mental illnesses are often misdiagnosed.

The psychiatrist's words were somewhat comforting. There really was a reason for all the trouble I'd had with my studies and relationships, and I could get help. My drug overdose? Probably a delayed reaction to all the stress I'd been under.

Everything seemed pretty overwhelming. But the next day, when friends brought my Bible and glasses, I felt better. I attended group therapy sessions to learn more about the disease. I even got to study some for my exams.

On Sunday, I was discharged from the hospital. In just the short time since I'd taken the medication, I had already noticed that the racing thoughts that had plagued me for so long were slowing down.

Healing

After graduation I moved in with a friend in a city closer to home and took the class I needed for my diploma. I was shocked at how much easier it was to concentrate on my studies, and I got a good grade.

In July I was offered a job in the town where my family used to live. I moved into my minister's guest room. His wife became a great source of strength and encouragement, and I could feel my faith growing as I did Bible studies with her.

> *I focus on all the positive things God has blessed me with.*

I knew that was where God wanted me to be. And when my symptoms increased, I was able to handle it with my doctor's prescription for a second medication.

I now live in a large city where I maintain my own apartment and work full-time. I'm consistent about taking my pills, meeting with my therapist, and seeing my doctor. Being bipolar also means I make sure I don't get too stressed. I've learned to watch my moods carefully so I can make adjustments to deal with them. I especially limit caffeine when I'm feeling manic, and

I avoid irritating situations and people as much as I can when I'm down.

But most of all, I focus on all the positive things God has blessed me with. Yeah, I've got a disease I have to deal with long-term. But God's given me the tools I need—loving family and friends, a job I like, a good church I'm actively involved in, and a great life that I can choose to thank him for every day.

by Jasmine Camps

I WAS SO HURT!

I couldn't find my name on the list. I didn't make the squad.

It was 11:58 AM. Just two more agonizing minutes until I would find out if I had made the high school cheerleading squad. I sat fidgeting in the hallway and waited impatiently for the announcement sheet to be posted. My stomach was doing flip-flops. Even though I'd been a cheerleader throughout middle school, I was nervous about making the squad.

"Hey, it's posted!" someone shouted.

We rushed to check the list. As my eyes scanned the sheet, my heart felt like it stopped beating. I couldn't find my name. I swallowed hard and looked again. It wasn't there.

Tears stung my eyes as I slowly backed away from the crowd. *How can this be*? I wondered in disbelief. Then, to make things worse, my best friend, Nikki, started jumping up and down and yelling, "I made it!" Her accomplishment felt like a smack in my face because *I* was the one who had talked *her* into trying out. As I watched Nikki celebrating with the other girls, I turned away and walked silently down the hall.

Why?

I went home that afternoon, my self-esteem shattered. I couldn't understand why God would take away something so important to me. I moped around the house for several days. Then one day my mom asked me a question that really stumped me.

"Have you considered that not making the squad might fit into God's plan?" she asked. "Sometimes it's hard to see the big picture, but God has reasons for everything. Do you really think he wants you to spend your time sulking?"

Her question made me realize how unfair I'd been with God. I had gotten so caught up with cheerleading that I hadn't been spending time nurturing my relationship with Christ. I decided right then that I was going to straighten out my priorities.

Over the next few weeks, I prayed and studied my Bible more. I also started participating in more youth group activities and became active in church drama. As I focused more on God, my perspective on cheerleading changed. Even though I still missed the energy of cheering, the activity didn't carry the same importance it once did.

Witnessing Opportunity

Then I was caught off guard when a unique opportunity came my way. Auditions were being held for an all-star cheerleading team, a non-school-affiliated squad that introduces girls to the world of competitive cheerleading. Nikki encouraged me to try out, but I felt torn. Although I enjoyed cheering, I didn't want to risk jeopardizing my restored commitment to God.

I shared my concerns with my mom, who offered a different perspective. She said it was unlikely all the girls on the all-star squad would be Christians. She told me this could be my chance to spread God's Word to people who hadn't learned of Christ's love.

My mom told me this could be my chance to spread God's Word.

It sounded great—in theory. But I always had attended Christian schools, and I wondered how hard it would be for me to step out of my comfort zone and approach nonbelievers. After several days of praying and asking for God's guidance, I decided cheering was a fantastic opportunity to share my faith.

So I tried out, and this time I made it. Immediately, I thought of what Mom had said about God's bigger plan. I felt sure I'd made the all-star squad rather than the school squad because God wanted me to witness to my new teammates. And that's exactly what I did.

Christ in Me

When the girls looked at my life, I wanted them to see Christ. So whenever I had to leave practice early to go to youth group, I was sure to tell everyone where I was going and extend an open invitation to anyone who wanted to join me. I also wore a lot of Christian T-shirts, which led to conversations about Jesus. And I always prayed before every competition. Most importantly, I just tried hard to demonstrate God's love by the way I acted.

Over time, I saw changes in my teammates. For instance, I noticed they stopped using profanity. Also, more and more girls joined me in the daily devotional meetings I led. These devotionals not only brought us closer as a team, they also gave the other cheerleaders a chance to learn more about God.

My teammates weren't the only ones who changed. I did too. I used to think that nothing could compare to the jazzed feeling I got when I cheered in front of packed bleachers. Now I've found something that feels even better—sharing Christ with others.

by Anne Williman

THE PAIN AND GAIN OF SUFFERING

For the first time, my illness looms over me like a monster.

It's 3 AM and the hospital's quiet, but I can't sleep.

Beside my bed, a six-foot gleaming metal pole supports a plastic bag connected to my vein by tubing. Though the intravenous needle in my arm doesn't hurt, the medicine flowing in through it burns. I watch the drops of antibiotic fall like reluctant raindrops into the tubing. Their slowness and the pain mean I'll need a new IV needle in the morning. With seven doses of strong drugs a day, my veins can't tolerate the invasion for long.

Carefully, so I won't disturb the IV, I turn over, refusing to look at the pole any longer. I hate the thought of the nurse stabbing my arm again with the vicious two-inch needle.

Oh, God, where are you? I pray. *Why is all this happening to me?* I long to be safe in my own home, with my family around me, instead of silently suffering in the dim light from the hospital corridor, which filters in through the half-shut door. I dread the approaching day.

For the first time, my illness looms over me like a monster, bearing no resemblance to the mere inconvenience it's been all my life.

Alone in the dark hospital room, I cry.

Fairly Normal Life

At the age of five, I was diagnosed with cystic fibrosis (CF), a lung and digestive disease. It had been inherited from my parents, who each unknowingly carried a gene for CF, although they didn't have the disease themselves.

It used to be that CF patients died at early ages, with doctors able to do little. But now advanced techniques to clear the airways can be done several times a day. Along with aerosol masks to breathe medicine, plenty of pills, and regular visits to a specialist, patients now live much longer, some into middle age. Lung transplants also have lengthened the life span of a number of people who otherwise would not have made it.

In my case, the disease was mild. I went through school living a fairly normal life in spite of all the extra treatment I had to go through. But I knew I could never have the kind of life my friends enjoyed, and I wondered why I had to be the one with the fatal disease.

At a youth retreat I talked about all this with Linda, one of our sponsors. She had been in a serious car accident, for which she was still receiving medical treatment. Linda told me she used to struggle with "Why me, Lord?" But, she said, she had reached the place of saying, "Why not me?" As a Christian, she felt she was better able to cope with her problem than an unbeliever would be. God had helped her accept the suffering in her life as something she could bear because he was there to help her.

> **I wondered why I had to be the one with the fatal disease.**

Years passed, during which CF was in the background of my life. Yes, I still did the treatments, saw my doctor and got the extra rest, food, and exercise I needed. But other problems and joys were in my thoughts, not the disease.

Until my health gradually began to change.

Why, God?

I began struggling with chronic fatigue and chest congestion. Nothing the doctor tried seemed to work, and I ended up hospitalized for two weeks with my family two hours away. It turned out to be one of the worst times of my life.

In addition to the physical pain, there was the emotional stress of seeing what the disease does in a far more personal way than I'd experienced before. Death wasn't the issue; I felt prepared for that. I knew my faith in Christ meant a place in heaven.

But I hadn't known much about the process a CF patient goes through to get to that point. In the hospital I found out. It was devastating. One girl had had so many IVs that she had no veins left in her limbs for the antibiotics to flow into. She had to get a permanent IV surgically implanted in her chest. Many others with CF couldn't hold jobs or live on their own. They were obviously moving closer and closer to death each day, and the path there was painful and slow, like some kind of medieval torture.

Oh, Lord, I can't go through all that! I prayed. And I was angry, more angry than I'd ever been.

It just wasn't fair. Why were CF patients dying? Why did the disease attack only children and young adults who had had so little chance to live? Why did the God of all creation do nothing as another person struggled to breathe, infection raging wild inside his lungs with doctors watching helplessly? What about all the other people in the world who suffered from illness, crime, and hunger?

The questions burned in me as much as the antibiotics dripping into my vein. If only this was all just a nightmare I could wake up from. . . .

Learning from Suffering

But after I left the hospital, the fury gradually faded, and my bruised body and battered emotions healed. As they did, the Lord quietly began assuring me of his love and compassion for each suffering person. He didn't resent my questions or anger. He even taught me some truths about suffering.

Everyone goes through pain in some way. No, it's not fair, because the burden of pain or sorrow is much heavier for some than for others. Compared to people like quadriplegic Joni Eareckson Tada, my suffering is minimal. Yet as Joni says in her book *A Step Further,* no one has the right to say someone else's problem isn't bad enough to hurt.

But though it's agonizing, God can use it. My pain shows me how much I need him, and it demands that I trust him more, even when I don't understand why I'm suffering. It also makes me more like Jesus, as through it I develop patience, endurance, and the ability to be content in all circumstances (Philippians 4:11). I'm promised in 1 Corinthians 10:13 that I'll never undergo more than I can handle.

> *The Lord quietly began assuring me that he didn't resent my questions or anger.*

Another benefit? Sensitivity to others' pain. Having suffered, I'm often very aware of hurting people around me. No one can relate to pain like someone who also has been through it. That fits with 2 Corinthians 1:3-5, where it says believers who have suffered have a responsibility to help others who suffer.

In the hospital I found that it didn't help when people quoted Bible verses or told me to have faith, even though they meant well and were right. I now know a hug and a listening ear is the best thing to give a hurting friend.

Suffering's never fun, but it is temporary (1 Peter 1:6, 7). And knowing that it can do good in my life makes it easier to handle. That doesn't mean I've enjoyed the additional hospitalizations or some of the other painful experiences I've had. But I do know that each time pain comes, Jesus will be there to get me through it.

Into the Light

When life was running out
and my cup was becoming dry,
you heard my silent shout;
you saw my painful cry...

You held me in your arms,
soothing me patiently,
calming all my alarms,
you gently help me see...

That without you I'm nothing,
and I have no purpose in life.
But you're here, with me,
and you've brought me into the light.

by Lynndie Wilhelm (written at age 16)

by Rosemarie DiCristo

UNANSWERED PRAYER

Why are my friends hurting? Why is God silent to their pain?

Some of my friends and relatives are going through really rough times. A cousin who I deeply love is seriously mentally ill. A close friend is being tormented by her boss. Another friend, an older one, has a bad neck injury which, if it progresses, can paralyze her.

I Don't Know

I've prayed, of course. Prayed desperately on my hands and knees, on the floor, the room dark, praying.

Nothing happened. Nothing positive, I mean. My cousin was institutionalized. My friend's job situation has gotten so bad she'll probably be fired. My other friend reinjured herself in an accident in her doctor's parking lot.

Why?

It's a question I'm asking God over and over. My friends are good people. Kind. Caring. Generous.

While my friend's boss, for instance, is cruel, vindictive, and completely lacking compassion.

Why are my friends hurting? Why is God silent to their pain? They're all Christians. They all believe. They're all praying for help—they and everyone we know. So why have their lives gotten worse?

I don't know.

I'll never know.

God Is God

I can get all intellectual and say that God is in control, that he knows what he's doing, that it'll all turn out for the best.

Honestly? Sometimes it's hard to be comforted by that.

Then again, what choice do I have?

God *is* in control. He does know what he's doing. He's God. God Almighty. God Most High. God.

He's God if I believe in him. He's God if I don't believe in him. Whatever I do, whatever I think, he's God, and always will be. That won't change.

If I can cling to that in the mess of everything else . . . well, it's still not the comfort I want because it doesn't solve things the way I want. But I do know God is always there, even when I think he isn't.

Maybe one of my prayers should be to find peace in that fact.

CAN I GET A DO-OVER?

"... Cheer up! On your feet! He's calling you."

—Mark 10:49

by Todd Casbon

BUSTED!

"Faster," my friends urged. I grinned smugly and pressed hard on the accelerator.

As we rolled up and down hills and banked sharp curves, I kept pressing the accelerator for more speed. I wanted to see how fast I could make Dad's Chevy go on this hilly and winding country road. It was like riding a roller coaster.

Since most of my friends didn't have their licenses yet, I was the cool guy who drove everyone around. So, of course, I had to show off whenever I could.

"Faster," my friends urged. I grinned smugly and pressed hard on the accelerator. At the crest of a hill, we went airborne and then the car quickly jolted back onto the road with a loud thud.

My friends went crazy.

"Yeah!"

"Awesome!"

Right after I cleared the top of another hill, my heart jumped as I spotted a cop car hidden behind some bushes. I'd caught the blurred shadow of a man pointing a radar gun out the window . . . right at me.

Instinctively, I slammed on my brakes and skidded past the officer as he fishtailed his car onto the road and sped up behind me with his lights flashing.

Busted.

Slowing Down

"You've gotta be kidding!" I groaned in frustration as my mom's warning echoed in my head.

"You'd better slow down," she had recently told me. "If you get a ticket, I'm confiscating your license."

Even when I was driving with Mom in the car, I had a tendency to push the speed limit. I'm sure she could only imagine how fast I drove when she wasn't around.

As the burly officer approached my car, ticket pad in hand, my stomach churned.

Mom and Dad are gonna kill me!

My heart pounded hard as I rolled down my window.

"Son, do you realize you were going fifty-nine in a thirty-five mile per hour zone?" the officer asked me in his deep southern drawl.

I desperately searched my thoughts for a reasonable excuse. Then it hit me. I remembered my driver's education instructor reminding us to watch our speed after leaving the highway. He had warned that an extended period of high-speed driving on the highway can make you *feel* like you're going slower than you really are. He even had a word for it that came to me—and just in time.

"Uh, I'm not sure . . ." I responded as I strained to keep my voice from quivering. "But I think I must have been *velocitized*."

The cop crinkled up his eyebrows and looked at me like I was crazy. Clearly, my brilliant excuse hadn't worked. When he handed me a ticket, my stomach dropped. I knew some older guys who'd gotten tickets from the county sheriff's department, and their parents had received a letter telling them all about what had happened. Now my parents would get a similar letter.

Great. I'm toast.

Keeping Quiet

As I drove home that afternoon—slowly—all I could think about was how to save myself. Save myself from the humiliation of having to tell my friends that my parents had taken my license. Save myself from the lecture I'd get from my dad, who, ironically, was a driver's ed teacher. Save myself from the painful and inevitable grounding that would surely follow. And I didn't want to be grounded because I had plans to go camping with friends. So I kept quiet.

That evening as my buddies and I sat around the roaring bonfire, we brainstormed ways I could intercept the letter before my folks saw it.

"For the next week, you *gotta* get to the mailbox before your parents do," Cole said.

"That's not gonna work," I replied. "They're both teachers. Some days Dad's home by 3:15."

"Well, is there anyone in your neighborhood you trust who could check the mail for you before your parents got home?" John asked as he tossed another log on the fire.

Someone I trust.

I couldn't help but get stuck on that word: trust. There we were, weeding through possible scenarios of how I could hide the truth from my family, and I was thinking of who I could trust to do something dishonest for me. It didn't seem right, but I kept those thoughts to myself.

I had messed up—not just by getting the speeding ticket but also by not telling Mom and Dad about it.

We stayed up late playing cards, eating junk food, and talking sports, but I couldn't enjoy myself. Guilt and shame washed over me. All I could do was think about how I had messed up—not just by getting the speeding ticket but also by not telling Mom and Dad.

Coming Clean

The next morning while my buddies were still sleeping, I went for a walk in the woods to be alone with God.

"Dear Lord," I prayed as I made my way down a dirt path. "I've messed up—big time. Of course, you already know that."

Bright sunshine streamed through the thick tree branches, reminding me once again of God's wonder and beauty.

"I'm so sorry for how I've been acting. When I got that ticket, I freaked out. I panicked and stopped thinking clearly.

"I'm sorry, God, for driving carelessly and for not being honest with Mom and Dad. Please give me the courage to tell them what I did. I don't want them to be ashamed of me, but mostly I don't want to disappoint you. Please forgive me, Lord."

That evening at dinner I took a deep breath and said, "Mom, Dad, I have something to tell you." I thought it would be best if I blurted it out quickly and painlessly, like ripping a bandage from your skin.

"I was busted yesterday for speeding," I said quietly. Mom looked at me with fire in her eyes.

Dad just nodded and said, "Your Uncle Roger mentioned that he saw you. He passed you when you were pulled over."

I braced myself for the third degree, but my parents' reaction surprised me. They were definitely disappointed, and they *did* take away my wheels for two months, but they also did something I wasn't expecting. After going on and on about how dangerous speeding is, they hugged me, thanked God for keeping me safe, and told me that they appreciated my honesty.

My parents' reaction surprised me.

I must admit, it felt good to tell the truth. And as far as my ticket, I lucked out. Because it was my first offense, I only had to pay the minimum fine. I also had to attend a six-week defensive driving course.

The sting of having to face my friends without a license was the toughest part. Without my car I was no longer the cool guy with the fast ride.

But that's OK. I've learned there is something better than that need for speed. It's the feeling that comes from acting in a way that pleases God.

by Jennifer Dunning

DADDY'S NOT-SO-LITTLE GIRL

Relating to God as my Father is a relationship I have always struggled to fully experience.

At the age of six I believed that praying harder meant clasping my hands tightly and squeezing my eyes shut. And that is what I did night after night while praying desperately for my daddy to notice me. To want to spend time with me. To love me. But those prayers seemed to continually go unanswered.

I grew up trying to do everything I could think of to be better. To be smarter. To be funnier. To be prettier. But it would never be enough to get his attention. Now, I have left behind those childhood aspirations of gaining the affections of my father.

A Relationship I've Never Known

If you happened to grow up with a dad like mine, you may agree with me when I say that movies like *Father of the Bride* are difficult to watch. This is a movie that shows a father so crazy about his little girl that he is crushed to realize she is all grown up and will be leaving him to get married. There are touching scenes where this father and daughter play basketball together and talk about all the memories they have of time spent with one another. I become uncomfortable watching movies like this because that type of relationship is one I have never known.

This is the part where you expect me to tell you that everything is different now with my heavenly Father, who has filled the void of my earthly father. Well, there is no denying that life with the Lord has filled the void in my heart, but relating to God as my Father is a relationship I have always struggled to fully experience.

An Exercise in Imagination

I went on a retreat recently that helped me more closely examine my relationship with God. I will challenge you, as I did, to do one of the exercises from that retreat. You'll need a few sheets of paper and some markers. Go gather your supplies and come back so we can get started.

Welcome back. Here we go. On the first sheet of paper, I want you to draw a picture of God the Father. You may think this is crazy since none of us have actually seen God. But take a few moments to think about how you visualize him during your prayer time and when you lift your voice in praise.

Is there an image or picture that comes to your mind? Draw it.

After you have completed your first masterpiece, take the next sheet of paper and draw a picture of Christ the Son. Draw him the way you see him in your mind.

Some of you may have drawn a picture of Jesus when I asked you to draw God. This is not uncommon.

If so, now try to draw the Father, again. See if you can portray two different images of God.

Then take a few moments to examine your works of art. What colors did you use and are they significant? What are the emotions exhibited in your picture? Where are you in the picture? Do you feel God is happy to see you or disappointed in you? This exercise can be very telling—not only how you see God but how you relate to him as well.

A God I Couldn't See

For me, this simple trip back to elementary art class came with a startling revelation about how I relate to God the Father. I picked up the markers and let the colors explode as I enjoyed sketching the images of my imagination.

But what I actually drew was Jesus the Son. When I was then asked to draw Christ the Son, since I had already done so, I had to try and focus my mind on drawing my mental image of our everlasting Father. As I sat there with a green marker in my hand, my mind was blank.

No color splashed across the page because I had no image of God as a Father.

After a lifetime of disappointment, I had convinced myself I had no need for a father.

I could understand Jesus as my Savior, my friend, my comforter, and my shepherd. But after a lifetime of disappointment, I had convinced myself I had no need for a father. Staring at a blank piece of paper that afternoon, I began to realize I had never learned to embrace God as my Father. Rather, I had never allowed him to embrace me as his child. I had not allowed him to fill that void for me. And I did not know how to begin such a relationship with the almighty God.

A Father I've Always Wanted

Later during that same retreat, everyone sat around a cross. We took turns having our feet washed. It was as I sat at the foot of that cross that I heard the Holy Spirit speak to me. My heavenly Father was whispering an apology on behalf of an earthly father who was never there for me.

Jen, I am sorry you have been hurt, and I am sorry you have felt so alone. I know the father you have always wanted to have and I AM. As I heard him speak those words to my heart, I began to weep.

The Father I thought I could live without had been there all along.

I am still learning what it is like to call upon God as my Father. My heart has been broken by my earthly father but healed by my heavenly Father. And it feels so good to be able to come to him like a child. And as Daddy's not-so-little girl, I can come to God with my hands clasped tightly and my eyes squeezed shut and let him love me with a love I have always wanted to have—and a love he has always wanted to give.

by Cindy Ooms

BEYOND ALL BARRIERS

I marvel at how God could look past so much terrible stuff and accept someone completely.

We live in an incredibly diverse culture. In one neighborhood you'll find every skin color, faith, and career choice. Each person, no matter his social standing, beliefs, or lifestyle, has his own set of problems. Cancer excludes no religion. Divorce invades every social class. Pain respects no boundaries. Death reaches every life. Fortunately, there is also hope that reaches beyond any barrier.

There are problems that money can't fix, friends can't alleviate, and no amount of counseling will mend. But there is no issue beyond the reach of Jesus' love.

No Ordinary Choir

I'm reminded of that fact every year when our church family is joined by a traveling choir for a Sunday. This is no ordinary choir. If you just walked in off the street, you'd wonder why they were up there because their vocal skills aren't always impressive. Notes are out of tune, and there is no harmony. But the members of this particular choir are involved because of what Jesus has done in their lives.

All of the choir members have pasts involving drug or alcohol abuse. Most have been through countless rehab programs—with no results. Many lost their families and jobs. Every last one, at some point, lost all hope of a better life. And then Jesus entered the picture.

At one time or another, these choir members stayed at Minnesota Teen Challenge, and their lives were changed. They were introduced to hope—real hope. Hope that lasts through tough times and through pain. Hope that lasts for eternity.

When the choir members share their testimonies, I am always amazed at the power of Jesus' love in people's lives. From a human perspective, these people are in the lowest class of society. If you want to talk about messed up lives, here you go. They have committed crimes not only against the public, but also against their families and themselves. These people gave up. But once Jesus entered their lives, everything changed! Many of them have gone into full-time ministry. They go back into society with jobs and skills. They will truly never be the same.

Lowest of the Low

Stories like these really make you think. Or at least, they sure make me think! They make me question my doubts about Jesus. I see God's faithfulness, power, and commitment to us in amazing ways. I marvel at how he could reach across such incredible barriers—how he could look past so much terrible stuff and accept someone completely.

Think about it! There are plenty of decent people around, people who haven't committed any crimes and are genuinely good citizens, just not Christians. Why doesn't God focus on them? Why does it seem like he pursues those who "just aren't worth it"? Even in the Bible it was like that. Jesus was always hanging out with the lowlifes of Israel.

Jesus reaches beyond any wall we work so hard to build.

But it's not the whys and hows that are important. The point is that he does—Jesus reaches beyond any wall we work so hard to build. No matter how far we run, he always catches up. The more we try to make ourselves unlovable, the more he loves us. The bigger the mess we've made of our lives, the more he is ready to forgive. Do you get it? You can try to convince yourself that you are the exception. You can keep telling yourself that you've passed the point of no return and forgiveness is out of the question—but that would all be a lie.

When we finally reach the point where we dare to ask Jesus to clean up our lives, nothing else matters to him. Our forbidding barriers are crushed. All our mistakes are thrown to the bottom of the deepest sea. Our tears are wiped away and our fears relieved. Life starts over, and it'll never be the same again.

If the only picture of Jesus you've imagined is one who points fingers and condemns, let me introduce you to the real Jesus. The one who sacrificed everything for you. The one who is waiting for you to come running home. The one who passionately pursues you. That's the Jesus I know, and it's the same Jesus that you can know.

There Was a Time

There Was a Time When
I Thought: "It" Would Make Me a Better Person
I Feared: Dying
I Avoided: Getting Caught
And I Pretended: That I Didn't Care
But I've Changed
Now I Remember: Who I Am
I Regret: Doing Drugs
I Regret: Getting Stoned
I Wish: I Could Start Over
I Hope: To Be a Better Person
Because Now
I Want: To Be Someone

by Jahade Brayboy (written at age 15)

GOD USES EVEN ME

God opened my eyes to see the seriousness of everything I was doing.

I was raised in a Christian home with an awesome family. My parents brought me up right and taught me to love the Lord with all my heart. I knew the Christian lingo. I knew what the Bible was about and went to church every Sunday.

As I got older, I started getting into sports. It's not like sports are bad, but as a result of them I started becoming popular. I wanted to test out the world a little bit, so, when I was fourteen, I started partying pretty heavily. I drank and did stupid things. Even though I knew the kind of life I should have been living—the kind my parents had raised me to live—I started to backslide.

When I was sixteen, I went to a Christian camp in California. While there, God spoke to my heart and said, "Jeremy, I want to use you. You have to stop what you're doing, this mess and junk you're involved in." He opened my eyes to see the seriousness of everything I was doing. I gave my heart back to the Lord.

Broken in Spirit

For a couple of years after that, I struggled some. I didn't go back to partying or anything. But I struggled with still having those desires in my heart.

After high school, I went to Bible college. During my first semester there, a pastor spoke a message about being set apart. I realized I had all this junk in my heart, filling my life. It was a point where I had to submit everything and just say, "Hey God, I just want to be yours. I'm broken before you." That's when I really feel like God gave me a new heart, when I was able to let go of all these things I clung to. I was still holding on to the world just a little bit.

At sixteen, I gave my heart to Christ after that moment at camp. But my first semester at college is when my spirit truly broke and I gave everything to God. I remember one night I cried for two hours. God just worked on my heart. It was awesome, pretty radical actually.

Nourished by the Word

When I went to Bible college, I didn't know exactly what I wanted to do with my life. I just wanted to go and learn the Word of God. I knew I wanted to be in ministry in some way, I just didn't know what it was. But I wanted to have that foundation in the Word of God. I knew that going out and trying to minister without that foundation would be slippery. It's not that you can't do it, but I wanted that wisdom in my own heart. I wanted to study the Word. It's our food for our souls. It's our nourishment. So I went to Bible college, studied from Genesis to Revelation, and it was amazing what God taught me. College was definitely a turning point.

I went through two full years. When I was done I started going to a church and leading worship. I began getting a lot of phone calls from different churches, the leaders saying, basically, "We want to hear what everyone has been talking about at Bible college. My son, my daughter, my youth group kid told us about you, so please come play at our church." That started happening a lot.

Pretty soon I started getting so many phone calls that I started leading worship and doing concerts full-time. I did a demo and sold ten thousand records within a really small amount of time. Eight months, actually. It was obvious that God was opening up the doors for me to play music.

Humbled Before God

Even though God has totally captured my heart, I still have lessons I'm learning. Something God has laid on my heart lately is going back to the foundation of why I'm here on this earth: to fellowship with the Lord. The greatest commandment is to love the Lord your God with all of your heart, soul, mind, and strength and to love your neighbor as yourself. I feel like God recently has been saying, "Jeremy, slow down. You've been so busy and just doing, doing, doing, and trying to take control of things and make this or that happen. Just rest in me. Remember when you were broken, and it was all about just hanging out with me."

For me to be effective in what God's called me to do I have to spend time with Jesus. From that time, the overflowing will be the compassion that I need, the fruit of the spirit. I need to go back to that simplicity. It's a lesson I hope I never forget.

God uses the foolish things of the world.

Music has opened doors to minister to many people. That's blown me away to see. To see what God's done, to see thousands and thousands of people who have responded because of how God's using me—that blows me away. It's very humbling, for sure.

It's been crazy to hear from around the world the stories from random people. I got a letter from Malaysia the other day, saying thank you for your music. It's crazy. I don't understand it because I know I'm an idiot.

But I also know that God uses the foolish things of the world. I'm proof of that.

by Christina Dotson

I LOST MY COOL

My fight wasn't the glorious achievement I imagined it to be.

For a long time I bragged about my very first fistfight. I told and retold the story to any friend who would listen. I thought it was something to be proud of.

The fight had been against three of my cousins. We were vacationing at the beach, and they had done nothing but torment me all day long. They dumped sand in my hair, threw my towel in the water, and tried to dunk me under every chance they got. Finally, I'd had enough.

When my cousins Brian and Justin splashed another huge spray of seawater in my face, I lost it. The next thing I knew I was kneeling on Brian's back, holding him underwater as I reached over and slugged Justin. My cousin Steven jumped on my back and I kicked him off. I was so furious I barely knew what was happening. My mother and two uncles had to drag us apart.

That'll teach them to mess with me, I thought. I was so proud of myself. I had held my own in a fight against three guys. I had every right to be pleased . . . didn't I?

It took me longer than it should have, but I eventually came to realize my fight wasn't the glorious achievement I imagined it to be. I had to learn the hard way the many reasons why uncontrolled anger is nothing to take pride in.

Uncontrolled anger makes you do things you'll regret.

After the fight with my cousins, my mother told me that she had been afraid I was going to drown Brian, since I had held him underwater for so long. What was even scarier, though, was that I didn't even *realize* what I was doing.

That's the problem with losing your temper—it makes you lose control of yourself. And when that happens, you may end up doing or saying terrible things you'll never be able to take back.

Uncontrolled anger makes a bad situation worse.

Fighting didn't fix anything between me and my cousins. It only made them torment me more . . . which of course led me to continue fighting. Before I knew it we were locked in a vicious cycle of anger and bickering. Neither side wanted to back down.

If only I had kept my cool in the first place, our feud probably wouldn't have lasted so long. This is why the Bible advises us to "refrain from anger and turn from wrath . . . it leads only to evil" (Psalm 37:8). Losing your temper will only make the situation go from bad to worse.

Uncontrolled anger destroys relationships.

The tension between my cousins and I eventually got so bad we could barely stand to be in the same room. Family get-togethers were always awkward. The four of us were all about the same age, so we should have been able to hang out. But our years of fighting had created a rift that took a long time to repair.

This is often what happens when you lose control of your anger—you lose the chance to share in some potentially great relationships.

There's nothing wonderful or exciting about fighting, either with words or fists. Even if you think you have good reason to do so, the consequences just aren't worth it.

In the long run, it's a whole lot smarter to just keep your cool.

Thank You

Here I am in your presence again
Hey I'm here, asking forgiveness again
Over and over I fell on my face
But you picked me up and stood in my place
You took on my pain and all my worst fears
You showed me true love and wiped away tears

You know all my dreams, my first waking thought
The scars that I hide and the battles I've fought
You've always been here, right by my side
Through the thick and the thin and the times that I cried

I remember a time when I laughed at your name
When I hid from the light and cowered in shame
A time in my life when I was unloved and alone
But you've blessed me with friends, and you gave me a home
You've shown me compassion and taught me to love

You're the gateway to heaven and my Father above
You brought a purpose to life, a reason to live
Nothing brings strength like the hope that you give
You're the grin on my face and the light in my eyes
You see the real me and none of the lies
The forgiveness you give is all that I need
With you in my life my soul has been freed
You came from the heavens to live in my heart
You were here before time, right from the start
Your death on the cross showed the meaning of love
You brighten our lives from the heavens above
You light up our paths and show us the way
You're here in my heart and that's where you'll stay
You're the Savior of souls and our saving grace
And all you require is having our faith

by BJ Hughes (written at age 16)

by Tennille Johnson

UNCONSCIOUS

My dad had been in an accident, and he was brain dead.

Like any other day, I came home from school and grabbed a quick snack and soda. I had a mound of homework, so it was time to get busy. But something seemed suspicious about the day. For one thing, it was a workday for my mother, but she wasn't going anywhere.

I went to my room and began my homework. About an hour later, my mother came in my room and said, "Slip on some shoes. We have to get somewhere quickly." As I fumbled with my shoestrings, we left quickly. Riding in the car I continuously asked my mom where we were going, but she wouldn't say. We arrived at the hospital, and I became scared because I knew it was something serious.

No Earthly Father?

Once we were inside, I began to notice a lot of my family there, as well as a local preacher. Still not knowing why I was there, a doctor came in and told our family the news. My dad had been in an accident in his work truck and hit his head. They ran CAT scans on him, and from what the doctors were seeing, he was brain dead.

When the doctor told us this news, all I could do was think, *I no longer have a father* and cry my eyes dry. I asked the doctor if I could see my dad, and he let me. My father was covered with so many machines and tubes it brought to mind a storm hiding beneath the clouds. The only thing I could do was grab his hand and pray. I spoke aloud in hopes that my earthly dad might also hear my voice.

Glimmer of Hope

The doctors decided to transport my dad to another hospital thirty miles away to have tests run on him. Once he arrived there, he was put in the Neurology ICU. He was hooked to a life support machine because he wasn't breathing on his own. At that point, at the age of fourteen, I had almost given up on having a father. I was also ready to give up on God.

They continued running tests on my dad and finally, for once, we received really good news: he was not brain dead. He'd had a stroke and was hemorrhaging from the brain. As months passed, I continued trying to communicate with my dad, letting him know someone was behind him, hoping for the best. I stayed out of school for about six months, spending nights in the hospital.

One day my father opened his eyes for the first time. He obviously couldn't talk because he had a trachea, but I could communicate to him and he could respond to me with facial expressions or his hands.

Welcome Home Party

Eight months later, we threw him a welcome home party. That was one of the best days ever.

This happened almost four years ago, and today my father doesn't get around too well and isn't able to do much for himself. He is still with us, though, and that's something I am thankful for every day. I try to see or call my dad for a few minutes every day to let him know I love him because I may not have tomorrow to tell him.

I've come to realize that you can't take even one day for granted.

From this life-changing experience I've come to realize that you can't take even one day for granted, nor can you let your relationship with God go astray. You could wake up and find your life changed forever.

For much of my life, I was unconscious of God's presence. Now I realize he has been there all along.

by Sarah Mae Ratliff

SCARED OF THE DARK

Here I am, walking on the trail, alone at night, scared out of my mind.

It gets dark here at least an hour before it does anywhere else. And once evening comes, it seems darker than any place I've ever been. The trees here grow so densely you're lucky if you can see the moonlight through them. The buildings also are spread so far apart that their lights are of little use when walking at night.

Dark Trail

I'm really not in such a dangerous place. I'm at church camp—the same church camp where I've spent all summer. I was here all last summer too. I've walked this same path at least six times today and probably hundreds of times before. I've led my group of campers on parts of this trail many times.

I have great memories of being on this trail. Often, we've raced up the path to make it to the worship service before anyone else. I'd often hurry my campers back down the path to their tents for rest time so I could have a short break. This is the trail that we'd sing songs on. This is the trail we'd use to go to the ropes course, the lake, or the pool. This is the path that led us to all the wonderful things that we could do at camp. I know that this trail isn't really hazardous. But for some reason, that knowledge doesn't make the walk any easier tonight.

I've never had the best eyesight at night. Other people excel at camp games that are played at night, like flashlight tag or capture the flag in the dark. Not me. But this is worse than a camp game. During the games, I know people are nearby. Right now, I can't see anything. Here I am, walking on the trail, alone at night, scared out of my mind.

I knew that this year I'd have to walk all the way from the camp office to the tents where the rest of the campers and counselors were. I guess I just didn't realize how long a walk it would be alone in the dark. After checking phone messages and making sure all the campers had the medicine they needed before bedtime, it's as dark as midnight.

Scary Obstacles

I should have asked to borrow a flashlight. Again. Each week I make sure my flashlight is ready and working. Each week, by the second night, it's broken or out of batteries. Tonight my flashlight has not yet broken, but the light keeps getting dimmer and dimmer. I have just enough light to see the ground right at my feet.

My heartbeat quickens along with my footsteps as I imagine all the things I could come across as I walk tonight. Could a stranger have come into the camp tonight? What will happen if I see a snake or raccoon?

Earlier this summer, I had been walking alone just before dark when I saw a long snake stretched across the side of the path. It wasn't so bad in the daylight. I moved to the other side of the path and hurried back to camp, even though I have an extreme dislike of snakes. Just remembering that snake made me shiver in disgust and fear as I walked alone. I hope there aren't any snakes out tonight. If I accidentally did come across one, by the time the light from the flashlight shone upon it, it would be too late to hurry away.

Needless Fear

If only I had a huge spotlight instead of a flashlight that is hardly working. If I had a spotlight instead, I'd know just where to go and I wouldn't need to be afraid.

You don't need to be afraid, I feel God's voice telling me.

I've been trying to walk alone on the path of my life.

This thought stopped me in my tracks. All summer I've been telling the campers that we can trust God because he is faithful to care for us.

Immediately, I begin praying as I walk. I ask God to forgive me for not trusting him. I feel myself become less and less afraid. I realize I don't need a huge spotlight instead of a flashlight. With my trust placed in God, I'll know just where to go and I won't need to be afraid.

Strangely enough, the woods now feel peaceful and beautiful as my small flashlight guides my steps.

You don't need to be afraid, I feel God telling me again.

And now I'm not afraid of walking on this path. I know that with God's help I can get where I need to go without a problem.

God's Flashlight

Finally, I make it back to the tents. The campers are nearly asleep.

I take out my journal and begin writing. Lately my journal has been a place where I list all my worries about school, family, and relationships.

You don't need to be afraid.

Then it hit me. I have been afraid. I haven't been completely trusting God. The realization of this gives me a sinking feeling, one worse than I've ever felt walking alone on a trail at camp. I've been trying to walk alone on the path of my life.

I looked back through my journal. Many of the things I needlessly worried about have been solved with God's help. God helped me with the little things like finding a dress to wear to a dance and the big things like getting enough money to go on a mission trip.

I've worried about far too many things. I've wanted to do it all and carry a spotlight on my shoulders to plan out each of my steps instead of just holding on to God's flashlight to lead me.

I turn to a new page in my journal and begin a new prayer:

Thank you, Father, that I don't have to be afraid. I'm choosing your joy instead of fear and worry. I don't need a spotlight; I need you. I'm asking you to direct my steps. . . .

by Jeanette Hanscome

WHEN FRIENDS FIGHT . . .

Some conflicts can't be solved neatly and easily.

I fought back tears as I hung up the phone. Kristen's hurtful words replayed in my mind. *Why didn't I do a better job of defending myself? What else could I say to someone who completely misunderstood something I had done? Did I just lose a friend?*

I spent that entire night in agony.

What is she saying about me to her family? How can she not see how wrong she is? If only I hadn't said . . . If only I had the guts to say . . .

How can I make her understand my side? God, please put it on Kristen's heart to call me back and apologize.

Somehow I knew it wouldn't happen. I'd have to make the first move.

What if I said something wrong, causing another fight? What if Kristen didn't want to talk to me? Should I just let the whole incident go and hope that we both get over it? Maybe I should avoid Kristen for a while.

No, we still had to see each other at church. More importantly, Kristen was my friend and sister in Christ. We had to work this thing out.

I tossed and turned all night, crying each time I thought of Kristen's insensitive comments and all the things I wished I'd done differently. But those sleepless hours gave me time to think and pray. My tears washed away emotion that might have driven our next conversation.

If I ignore it, it'll go away . . . right?

By the time Kristen and I talked, we had both cooled off and put things in perspective. It wasn't exactly a fun or easy conversation. I came right out and told Kristen that her comments had hurt me, and she let me know how my actions had affected her. This time, though, I hung up wiping away tears of healing instead of tears of frustration and anger.

Trying to Avoid the Issue

It was a good lesson, showing me that conflict doesn't have to destroy a friendship. It was a rare occasion when I actually faced an argument head-on. Usually I avoid conflict like bad coffee or people with the stomach flu.

Unfortunately, conflicts between friends happen. We have differences of opinion and do things that make each other mad. The question is how to solve these difficulties in a godly way.

If I ignore it, it'll go away . . . right?

For those of us who cringe at the thought of confrontation, the first response may be to run. Avoid the person. Say what he or she wants to hear to avoid an argument. Pray that God will work everything out so we won't have to deal with it.

That's exactly how I handled a disagreement with my friend Stephanie, which followed the conflict with Kristen. Actually our "disagreement" had been simmering for several months, waiting to boil over. We knew we weren't seeing eye-to-eye on some things, but neither of us wanted to sit down and talk about our differences because we hated conflict so much.

One day the issue came up in a conversation. After months of bottled-up resentment, we ended up having what we both feared—a major confrontation. We'd had way too much time to think about who was right and who was wrong. I walked away wishing we hadn't waited so long to address the problem.

I learned the hard way that ignoring conflict only gives the enemy time to work.

Calling for Reinforcements

A few days after my heated conversation with Stephanie, I went to one of our ministers for advice. I gave him a brief summery of what was going on with "a friend of mine." He gave me good biblical advice, and I went home with confidence to approach Stephanie again.

To my shock, not only did the minister's suggestions not work right away, Stephanie also got mad when I let it slip that I'd gone to him. Later I wished that I'd talked to her before making my appointment with the minister. I wished I'd suggested, "Let's talk to him together."

Not Alerting the Media

Mutual friends caught on to what was going on and tried to get involved, but I refused to add to the trouble by gossiping and trying to get friends on my side. When I talked to the minister, I kept Stephanie's name and any revealing information out of the conversation.

Venting to friends may feel like good therapy while dealing with a conflict. But as I had to remind myself many times, resorting to gossip—which God clearly hates—only leads to more problems down the road.

Knowing When to Let It Go

It frustrated me that the conflict with Stephanie wasn't working out like the one with Kristen. Eventually I had to accept that I'd done everything in my power to settle our differences. I finally had to lay the whole situation in God's hands—including my relationship with Stephanie.

I've found that letting go and giving up are two different things. Some conflicts can't be solved neatly and easily. They take time—time apart for God to work on each heart individually.

Seeing God's Work Pay Off

You can imagine my surprise when, more than a year later, Stephanie called me out of the blue.

"Jeanette, I need to ask your forgiveness," she said.

For the first time we were able to talk about what happened.

"It wasn't all your fault," I could finally admit. "I need to ask forgiveness too."

God had worked on both of us during those many months. He had taught us, through separate life experiences, what is important and what isn't. The issue that had once seemed so huge suddenly seemed like a silly thing to nearly end a friendship over.

It's amazing what can happen when we truly trust God with a problem and leave it with him. Often he does what we wanted in the first place—he works it out. The trick is allowing God to do it his way and in his timing.

by Andrew Parker

"IT WILL BE OK"

We'd escaped cancer's grip . . . or so we thought.

My mom had cancer. But after six rounds of chemotherapy, it appeared her lymphoma had gone into remission. After months of stressful living, our family quickly and excitedly returned to regular schedules and activities.

I could finally sit in class without wondering how Mom was feeling. Dad resumed his normal workload, and my brother, Joey, and sister, Sara, were relieved of their extra household chores. A summer vacation to the backwoods in our home state of Wisconsin invigorated us all.

The most memorable vacation moment occurred while trailing behind an all-too-powerful *Ski Nautique* speedboat in an inner tube. There's always something that happens to my mild-mannered father when placed behind the wheel of too much horsepower on the open water! Perhaps he sees an opportunity to repay me for all my dirty diapers and missed curfews over the years.

With the throttle buried, Dad whipped me around like a rag doll. My screams reverted back to the sounds of my prepubescent years, but I was determined not to let go. Unknowingly, my swim trunks started splitting from all the water pressure and my posterior became exposed for all the lake's sunbathers to see. This really "cracked" up my family. After months of living under a cloud of discouragement, laughter finally had returned to our household. We'd escaped cancer's grip . . . or so we thought.

Suspicions Confirmed

During Thanksgiving weekend, Dad and I noticed mom laboring more than usual during routine tasks. Laundry started piling up. Mom asked us kids to do certain jobs that usually were off limits, and by December she began asking Dad to help her up the stairs each night before bed.

A return trip to the doctor confirmed our suspicions. Mom's cancer had returned.

I grew up in Osh Kosh, Wisconsin, until my dad was transferred to Fort Wayne, Indiana, prior to my sophomore year of high school. I had always envisioned my life the way every kid does. My youth was spent re-enacting Super Bowl moments from the glory days of the Green Bay Packers. My middle school years included a crusade to catch every largemouth bass in the state of Wisconsin. High school was the usual smorgasbord of Friday night football games, way too much homework, and playing cards with my buddies into the wee hours of the morning. As for my future, I assumed I'd get married, have kids, and frequently dump them off at Grandma and Grandpa's for hours of adventure like I enjoyed growing up.

Some things just don't work out as you plan them.

On Monday, January 17, 2005, when her breathing

became quite erratic, we rushed Mom to the hospital. The doctors gave her three months to live. To our shock, Mom went home to Jesus by Wednesday of that same week.

Doctors gave her three months to live, but Mom went home to Jesus by Wednesday of that same week.

Life Changed

Life changed immediately for our family. In a short breath, I no longer would hear the calming voice say, "It will be OK" after a hard day at school. There was no one around to fix me a quick bowl of cereal as I ran behind schedule getting to school.

Mom's eyes would not be there to share a glance as I walked across the graduation stage.

But amidst the pain, I found strength in my faith. All the knowledge gained from sermons, church camps, and youth events was put into action, and I sensed God's presence. His love wasn't just phrases in a song or words on a page. It was real. It was evidenced in meals delivered by friends, hugs exchanged with family, and a youth group that planned my graduation party.

God's love also was given to me by my Youth for Christ director. In a time when I could have selected negative ways to grieve, he met with me weekly. He related to my life in a genuine way, while at the same time being another adult in my life that I needed. I even asked him to be a pallbearer at my mom's funeral.

Faith Secured

In spite of the hurt, I am so thankful for the family, friends, and faith that have seen me through. God used the death of my mother to turn my focus outward. I was forced to live each day by faith.

Teenagers are known for being risk-takers, but often in the wrong areas. Driving fast or skipping class are risks I ashamedly admit to, but nothing has proven more satisfying than taking the risk of placing my faith in an unseen God. Uncertainty combined with blind faith in Jesus has transformed my life, and I'll never be the same.

As for my future, I plan on attending Marquette University in Milwaukee. After that I'd like to own my own business. I'm sure a family is somewhere down the road, and one day I'm confident I'll once again hear, "It will be OK," as Mom and I stroll the streets of eternity.

You Found Me

I sought you at a distance.
I looked for you in knowledge.
And though I grasped the spoils of this world,

My heart was ever longing
As I groped in this meaningless state,
My soul trembling.
What is it that I lack?
When the point of desperation threatened to overtake me,
A glimmer of hope shone through.
My sorrow changed to gladness,
My guilt was transformed to peace,
And I found you.
I found you not at a distance.
I found you not in knowledge.
Though I grasped the spoils of this world,
You found me.

by Raschelle J. Minner (written at age 18)

by Maria Southman

A LIVING HOPE

The picture of the resurrection made my heart leap with joy.

When I was a kid, I used to love looking at the pictures of Jesus in my children's Bible. One was a glorious illustration of him right after the resurrection. He was robed in white, looking up into the sky with chestnut hair glowing, arms raised in victory.

Unlike the picture of the crucifixion, this one made my heart leap with joy.

Central to Our Faith

The crucifixion is central to our faith and salvation. But its significance is lost without the resurrection. Paul tells us in 1 Corinthians 15:14-17 that if Christ has not been raised, our faith is useless and futile and we are still in our sins. And if we can't believe that he'll raise us to join him after our own deaths, that if "only for this life we have hope in Christ," then "we are to be pitied more than all men" (1 Corinthians 15:19).

It's never been Jesus' physical resurrection or the physical resurrection of believers that I've had trouble believing—after all, it's God we're talking about here. But I often resign myself to being still in my sins (verse 17) and forget that Christ's resurrection means my resurrection as well.

Paul talks in Philippians 3:10 about knowing "Christ and the power of his resurrection." It's easy for me to forget that I have that same power and that I already spiritually have died and been resurrected along with Christ. It's easy to forget that sin is a choice.

I have so much trouble remembering Jesus' victory and living in the freedom he's given me. So often I expect sin and failure from myself, and I just rely on grace to catch me. But I forget what Christ died for, and rose for: to give me freedom. Because Jesus triumphed over sin in my place, I triumph over sin through him. So why don't I claim that triumph for myself? I will probably never be perfect, but I have every reason to hope that I will.

Angry with God

I'd like to tell you a little about my personal journey toward the hope Christ's resurrection gives. I've been a Christian practically all my life. But a few years ago, shortly after entering the confusing world of college, I went through some growing pains.

I was angry with God for creating the world. I couldn't believe that all the injustice and pain and the existence of hell as a final destination for some was a just trade-off for a few to enjoy heaven. I was even angry I was born without a say in the matter: how fair was it for God to create me and then demand love or eternal punishment?

For a few days I tried to ignore God, but the desolation was more than I could bear. I couldn't live without hope or without sensing God's love. Without him I was stuck with my miserable self, without purpose or joy.

I just couldn't stop loving God. I couldn't stop loving God because, despite my concerns, he had thrown himself into our mess to rescue us. Jesus ate, played, cried, and talked with us. And he died for us. And then he rose again to show us what the power he's given us looks like.

I just couldn't stop loving God.

Without his rising, what would his former actions have been worth? We would still be slaves to our sin, and our God would have been proven powerless. Hebrews 2:14, 15 puts it this way: "Since the children have flesh and blood, he too shared in their humanity so that by his death he might destroy him who holds the power of death—that is, the devil—and free those who all their lives were held in slavery by their fear of death."

This should give us much hope—we are no longer slaves to sin or death, which means anything is possible! As for my former wrestling matches with God, I can now say with Peter, "Praise be to the God and Father of our Lord Jesus Christ! In his great mercy he has given us new birth into a living hope through the resurrection of Jesus Christ from the dead" (1 Peter 1:3).

by Caroline Biggerstaff

A LIFE-CHANGING EXPERIENCE

God was the only one who could take away my dad's desire for drugs. But he avoided God.

Scared is the way I felt on sleepless nights. Screaming and yelling are things I heard most of the time for many years. Sometimes I would lie in bed and cry tears of heartache, hoping one day all the trauma would end. I felt my life would end if there was no way my dad would ever get off drugs.

Addiction

My dad started hanging out with the wrong people at a young age. Gangs and fights were things he was frequently involved in. He felt his life would be better, and he could have the satisfaction he desired, from drugs. He started drinking, smoking, and using crack cocaine, trying to fulfill his naturally sinful desires. What he didn't know was there were harmful consequences to each of those activities. His main addiction was crack, and there was only one thing that could stop his urge for the drug.

Being raised in a Christian home, my dad knew God was the only one who could take away his desire for drugs. But he avoided God, wanting his worldly pleasures instead. Any extra money he had, he spent it on drugs and wasted his life away. He even took Christmas money to try to satisfy his urge. He went as far as doing stupid things like robbing people to supply his need. Then he ended up in jail for eighteen months—but even that, and rehabilitation, couldn't help.

After my dad got out of rehab, he knew the desire was coming back, and he wished he could go back and change his life. But it was too late. Only God could help him.

Later, he joined a church where he hoped to get what he needed to control his life. He began talking to the pastor, asking him for advice on how to be saved. The only thing the pastor could tell him was, "Believe with all your heart and God will save you."

Redemption

After some halfhearted attempts, my father finally allowed Jesus to take hold of his heart and he became obedient to Christ as his Savior. My dad's life has been changed ever since.

It's almost like he is a new person. He now can tell others who are in that position that drugs will get you nowhere. They will ruin you forever. He witnesses to others on how to be saved. He is a deacon and teaches Sunday school. He also goes to the jail on Sundays and tells others what God has done for him.

This is an important lesson in my life. It's taught me that all drugs will do is ruin me forever.

I am thankful to have such a caring father to tell me about Jesus. I just wish everyone could understand how great God is—and how he can turn around any life.

by Christina Dotson

T-SHIRT TESTIMONY

I knew I wasn't behaving like a Christian. Yet I convinced myself that it didn't matter.

On a bright spring morning that seemed like a hundred other mornings, my alarm failed to ring and I woke up late for school. Frantically I threw on a pair of jeans and a T-shirt and ran downstairs.

Right away I knew this was going to be one of those days when everything goes wrong.

Bad Attitude

"Why didn't you buy more milk?" I demanded of my mother when there wasn't enough for a single bowl of cereal. I then proceeded to snap at my kid brother for eating the last of the frozen waffles.

Once at school, I realized I had forgotten my algebra homework. When my teacher asked about it, I replied with a smart-aleck comment. My teacher stared at me for a long moment, then shook his head and walked away.

In science class we had a pop quiz I wasn't prepared for. Feeling only slightly guilty, I accepted a friend's offer and copied the answers off his paper. *It was only worth a few points anyway,* I told myself. *It's not a big deal.*

At lunch, a girl accidentally spilled chocolate milk on my new sneakers. "Watch what you're doing!" I exclaimed, ignoring her apology. "What are you, a three-year-old?"

I needed to relax after a day like that, so I went to the movies with my friends. Once at the theater, however, someone suggested that we should try to buy tickets for an R-rated movie. The workers were too busy to check our IDs, so we easily got in to see a very violent and sexually explicit film. Once again I had doubts about what I was doing. I knew I wasn't behaving like a Christian. Yet I convinced myself that it didn't matter. After all, who was I hurting?

Only then did I notice the T-shirt I had carelessly thrown on that morning.

It wasn't until late that night, as I got ready for bed, that I realized how much my actions throughout the day really *did* matter. For only then did I notice the T-shirt I had carelessly thrown on that morning. It was a T-shirt I had received at a church youth retreat, and it had the entire Lord's Prayer written across the front.

My heart dropped to my stomach as I thought about how I had been behaving all day—snapping at people, talking back, making bad choices—all the while wearing a shirt that proclaimed I was a Christian. Without even realizing it, I had been dishonoring God's name from the moment I got dressed.

Bad Example

When we think about misusing the name of the Lord, we often think of using it as a curse word. Yet there are many other ways to dishonor God's name. Every time we go to church, pray in public, carry a Bible, talk about our faith, or do anything else that declares us as followers of God, we become representatives of his name. And when our actions contradict what we claim to believe, we bring disgrace to the Lord's name.

I shudder to think what my algebra teacher must have thought of me as I wore my Lord's Prayer T-shirt while talking back to him. And what sort of message was I sending my friends when I agreed to cheat on the science quiz and watch an inappropriate movie? I was a walking billboard for God that day, just as we all are when we profess to have Jesus in our hearts. My T-shirt should have been a testimony of my faith, yet instead of uplifting the Lord's name, I brought only dishonor.

The next time you clothe yourself in God's name, make sure your actions match your claim to Christianity. Only then can you truly honor him.

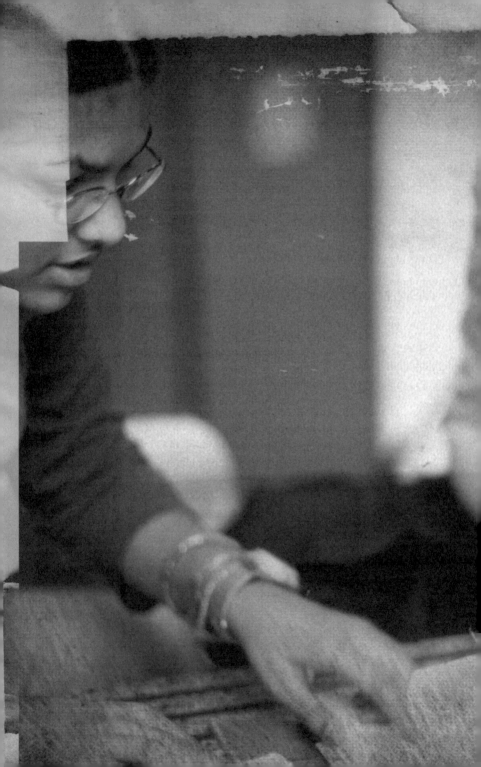

I'LL SHOW YOU HOW

"This is he who was spoken of through the prophet Isaiah: 'A voice of one calling in the desert, "Prepare the way for the Lord, make straight paths for him."'"

—Matthew 3:3

by Abby Conley

LOOKING FOR GOD

Sara wanted to talk to God, but when she was in so much pain, she couldn't find the words.

A couple of years ago, I had the opportunity to take a short-term mission trip to a Native American reservation in Arizona. There I met a fourteen-year-old girl named Sara. During the week, I learned a lot about her and a lot from her.

Sara's Family

Like many people on the reservation, Sara's life had not been easy. She came with some other teens to the service we were holding. Every night we played games, sang songs, had a message, and then met in small groups.

Sara said so much that week that no one ever could have guessed by looking at her. She seemed beautiful and happy. Instead, she was scared.

Sara's parents were around but did very little for her. Her father often disappeared for days, usually returning home drunk. At night, Sara often lay in bed and would hear her mom crying. Once, while looking for something in the hall closet, Sara found a box of letters her mother had written. Some threatened suicide; others just talked about how sad she was.

Sara had a brother who was almost twenty years old. She wished he could help her, but he had been in jail for the last few years. She said he was coming home in a couple more months, but that was even scarier because she didn't know what he would be like.

Lilly, Sara's younger sister, also came to the church that week. She was two years younger than Sara and just as trapped. Sara was sure God loved her younger sister more because Sara felt Lilly was prettier and smarter.

An Empty Sky

But Sara's greatest fear wasn't about her mother or father or brother or sister. Often, at night, when she didn't want to listen to her mother's crying anymore, she would climb out on the roof of their home to look at the stars.

The sky in Arizona is huge, and at night the desert is cool. There are almost no lights besides the stars, so they appear much brighter than they do in cities.

When Sara talked about the stars, she cried because she didn't think they were pretty. They reminded her of times when she went out on the roof to pray, but couldn't; she always felt as if she were talking to an empty sky. Sara wanted to talk to God, but when she was in so much pain she couldn't find the words.

Sara was like Job in many ways. She believed in God and wanted to serve him but didn't know how, because it seemed God had abandoned her. And, as with Job, Sara's family and friends didn't offer any help. Most of the people she knew didn't believe in God or Jesus.

Few people have as many problems in their lives as Sara did. Some may have brothers and sisters who stay in trouble or parents who really don't care what their children do. Some may know only one person who believes in God or may not have a church in their community. But few have all these problems together.

But Sara persevered. Even when she didn't feel as if anyone was listening or she couldn't pray because she was too upset, she looked for God. She knew he was there, even if she couldn't see or hear him. The idea that one day he would answer her helped her keep trying.

On the last night of the trip, no one really wanted to leave because we all knew that if we ever did see each other again, it would be a long time. But Sara said one thing before she left—it's remained with me since.

"I prayed last night," she said. "Nobody answered, but I'll keep trying."

THE POWER OF A MENTOR

As I got older, she made me realize the importance of mentoring girls.

Growing up, there was a woman in my church who I thought was really beautiful and talented. I really respected and looked up to this woman. When she took an interest in me, I felt thrilled. She would do small things with me, like comb my hair, and those acts of kindness meant the world. Best of all, she believed in me and my singing. Because she believed in me, she gave me belief in myself.

As I got older, she made me realize the importance of mentoring girls. Today, because of her influence, I've started what I call the Baby Girls Club.

Big Sister

The Baby Girls Club meets at my house in Franklin, Tennessee, and is meant to be a safe and comfortable place for young girls from the ages of nine to fifteen. We get together once a week on Wednesdays.

We have fun eating and dancing, but also it's a place to learn new skills like sewing and knitting. We normally do homework first and some kind of craft. We also do Bible memory verses. It's a place where the girls can be themselves and discuss what's going on in their lives. I kind of act as a big sister mentor to them.

The club has a diverse group of girls, some from the suburbs and some from the hood. They all have different family backgrounds, different interests, different personalities. Some know Christ and others are just getting to know him. Even though we have different people from different walks of life coming together, for two hours we're all baby girls.

I love these girls because they help me celebrate life and youth. I love their honesty, and we talk about everything. We talk about family, boys, clothing, homework, boyfriends—or lack of. When you talk to them with respect, you get respect.

They call me Aunt Bubbles. We have a friendship. We go shopping—either in my closet or to the mall. They inspire me and keep me in line. They challenge me in faith.

A New Look at Parents

One thing I talk to the girls about a lot is getting along with parents. You have to try and see where your parents are coming from. I remember what it felt like to get into it with my mom. We'd go around in circles.

My mom and I never had awful times, but we did go through points when we weren't best friends. I had to consider that she was married at sixteen, and by the time she was twenty-three she had three kids. She grew up with her kids. When I remember that, it helps me cut her some slack. She never went to a prom. She never was a kid. I had to consider all the facts.

> *Ask God for the compassion to help you see your parents as he sees them.*

I've spoken to a lot of teens about keeping their hearts free from bitterness. It's an epidemic. If you don't learn to forgive and let go, then you'll become what you hate in your parents. Your bitterness will direct you in that path. It's not that you won't be hurt, but let go of your right to revenge.

Help your parents, and then free yourself so you can continue to grow as a Christian, as well as in life. I've seen those who are able to forgive and walk away in freedom. It's one of the hardest things you ever have to learn. Is it fair? Maybe not in our standards.

Ask God for the compassion to help you see your parents as he sees them. Even though they're older, they're just grown-up teenagers. You have to ask yourself: what were your parents' teen years like?

Different Experiences, Same Emotions

I've had turning points in my life. That's life itself—good relationships, bad relationships, good decisions, bad decisions. Those things *are* life. Sometimes people think because you have a certain occupation you're immune, but it rains on the just and the unjust. The good news is that we have an umbrella, a protection, and that's Christ. We can learn from bad decisions.

For about three years I was physically abused in a relationship. I remember crying out to God for help. He brought people into my life to help and support me. I also realized that I had to forgive myself and my abuser because otherwise, I'd be full of bitterness and rage. With God's help, I was able to forgive and free myself from the chains of anger.

I tell people that, really, our situations and our experiences may be different, but the emotions every human feels from them probably are identical. We've all been ashamed, betrayed, elated, proud. We all have similar emotions where we can meet and say, "I've been there. I haven't walked in your shoes, but let's talk about how Christ has helped us through those times."

In my heart or in my actions, God has remained faithful. It's not about how good we've been because I haven't been good. Even on my best days, I've been bad.

If I can share with the younger generation just a speck of the hope and encouragement I received from my mentor growing up, then God will have used me.

For me, it's not about being a singer or songwriter or dancer. It's about loving people and being real.

Never Know

I might never know
Why you chose me
I might never know
What you'll give me next

I might never know
How much of a difference
I make in someone's life
By just being a friend

I might never know
How a simple "Hello"
Can brighten someone's day
When they are sad and alone

I might never know
Why you put me
Where I am
To do your work

I do know
That you have a plan
That I am involved in
To share your great love with others

by Elizabeth Prosise (written at age 15)

by Nicholas Farr

NOTHING TO FEAR

At first, I was scared to have a Muslim friend.

Waking up to a loud voice echoing through the air can be frightening—especially if you are in a Muslim country! My time in Bosnia and Herzegovina over two summers has been filled with many surprises. Some of these experiences were shocking, like hearing the call to prayer five times a day from a loudspeaker at the local mosque. Even though I was reminded daily of how different my summer home was, God liberated me from my misconceptions about Islam and having Muslim friends.

Out of My Comfort Zone

I went to Bosnia for an internship because I was majoring in missions at a Bible college. Originally, I did not want to go. I had mixed feelings about interacting with a belief system that was constantly in the news since 9/11. My family and I were very scared of the unknown, but God had other plans for my life. He quickly showed me that to give my life to him meant not only receiving Jesus but sharing what I have found.

Bosnia is roughly the size of West Virginia and has less than four hundred Christians. But one thing that always made me feel comfortable is how much Bosnia looked and felt like my home state of Tennessee. The beautiful hills and the attitudes of the Bosnians were both very inviting. Making friends in Bosnia was easy because it appeared the youth were excited to make relationships. Guys like my good friend Amir were always interested in how much we were alike. Daily, Amir would say he was amazed at the similarities in our two worlds.

At first, I was scared to have a Muslim friend—afraid I would do something wrong or scare him off. The more I watched our friendship, though, the more I saw God moving. God worked through our coffee shop moments and while we watched German TV. Once I got over being scared that I would offend Amir, our friendship developed easily.

I don't know what I expected. Maybe that it would be hard since I was an American, but that was not the case. All my friendships developed much smoother than I had anticipated.

"Minister That Was Different"

Amir asked one day what I was going to college for. Shocked and excited, I told him I was majoring in how to help people. Amir is a smart guy, and I think he already knew that I was interested in helping people since I had left home to come to Bosnia. I also think Amir already assumed that I was a Christian. (I have found that people usually associate being a Christian with being an American.) Amir did not seem to care about that, though, which was a relief to me!

I think we all feel scared about how people will interact with us once they find out we are believers—this time was no different. But God showed me again that he was in control and reassured me I had nothing to fear.

Amir and I became very close, and we shared our history and experiences. The second summer, when I was once again in Bosnia, he asked me if I was a minister. I told him that I was ordained, or "officially made a minister," in May. Amir stared at me for about five minutes while I waited, and I worried that I had gone too far in talking about religion.

To my relief, he looked at me and smiled. He said, "I have never met a minister like you. I like that." From then on, to everyone who Amir introduced me to, I was the "minister that was different" friend.

> *He said, "I have never met a minister like you. I like that."*

Looking back on our conversations, I find Amir was most shocked that I would leave my comfort zone and actually seek out a friendship with a Muslim. I am sure he knew all the bad news that has been circulated in America about Muslims and the fear that comes with that news. I believe Amir saw me as a different person because I *was* different.

I wanted God to show me how to see with his eyes, to see his depth of love for the Bosnian people. For me to pray those words daily were dangerous—to do so would place my heart at risk of being hurt. Thankfully, our God is not a God of hurt or pain! He chose to bless me in ways I will never fully understand—but can only experience in my friendship with Amir.

God showed me that he had amazing plans for a nation filled with followers of Islam.

God revealed to me that he wants to make a difference in the lives of people whose religion gives them no hope. He showed me that he had amazing plans for a nation filled with followers of Islam. He showed me just how crucial the cross was and how precious our freedom is because of Jesus' blood. God not only reshaped how I thought about Muslim friendships but also encouraged me to set aside my fear and step with him into the unknown.

Liberate Your Fears

I believe God wants to do similar things in your life. God wants to liberate you from your fears and misconceptions. Fear is not from God—hope and freedom await you.

But before you head out and walk by faith, I thought it best to give some practical advice. By all means, this is not all you need to know in having Muslim friends, but they are ways that God chose to work through me over two summers.

1. Realize you already have a lot in common with followers of Islam. Even though we read different books for our faith, we share a lot of history. Did you know Muslims believe that Jesus was a good man and performed miracles? We even share some cultural history. We both celebrate holidays and meals for fellowship.

Start with your common ground and then ask questions. Don't be afraid to be curious. Your Muslim friends will usually see this as a sign that you care. Live a life of evangelism.

2. God has provided you with the perfect opportunity to share your hope. Islam does not offer the same hope that we have in Jesus through the cross and the empty tomb. Muslims will work their whole lives not knowing the outcome once they die. We have confidence in knowing that we are secure in the salvation Jesus brings.

Let that show through your lifestyle. You can do this without being churchy. Do not force conversations about God; just show Muslims how much hope you have. The best advice is to just be you—God will do the rest!

3. Pray! Ask God to show you—with his eyes— how to view people who are different from you. God loves all of his creation and wants to use you in practical ways. Ask him to teach you what to say and show you how to love the way he loved. Go back and read about the activities of Jesus around all kinds of people. Use him as your example!

Have fun being God's hands of hope and feet of good news in your community!

by Tammy Darling

AN UNLIKELY FRIENDSHIP

She had everything I seemed to be lacking—and it made me sick!

She came into my life when I least wanted it but most needed it. I saw—rather heard—her while at a mutual friend's house. Her loud laughter carried across the room and continued throughout the afternoon. I began to find it really annoying. *No one can be that happy*, I thought. I was wrestling with God at the time and wanted nothing to do with happy people.

She Really Cared

Because I had recently started attending the same small church that she did, contact was frequent and unavoidable. She was outgoing, joyful, patient, and ready to serve at any time. She had everything I seemed to be lacking—and it made me sick!

God, however, knew she was just what I needed. She began to take interest in my life, and I could tell it wasn't superficial; she really did care. I was shocked!

I'd had such awful thoughts about her, and she really cared about me. My heart began to soften.

Over the weeks and months to follow she would ask how I was doing and let me know she was praying for me. Slowly I began to open up to her. Her laughter became refreshing and her servant's heart was beginning to rub off on me.

No One I Trusted More

A time came when I needed some counseling with our minister for a serious and private childhood issue, and my minister wanted someone there with me. I suddenly realized there was no one I trusted with this issue as much as I trusted her. She was there for me during a very painful time, and I'll be forever grateful.

Recently she drew my name as her "secret sister" in our church's encouragement ministry. She especially blessed me at Christmas with the (secret!) gift of a handmade blanket. I had been suspecting all along she was my secret sister and it turned out she was. I hope that someday I get to have her as mine.

It still amazes me how God used this unlikely woman to bless and change me. She was not someone I would have chosen as a friend—I initially thought she was loud, strange, and a fake. She was also much older than I was. I didn't think we would ever be friends. Thankfully, God thought otherwise.

Through this new and unexpected friendship I've learned to never judge people by how they look, sound, or act. This woman means more to me than she'll ever know. I just hope I can be as good an example of true friendship to her, and others, as she is to me.

by Natalie Watts

THE TOUCH

Many people around us today need the touch of love and acceptance.

Jesus set an amazing example the day he healed a leper—not just because he healed him but because he touched the man. Many people around us today need that same touch—the touch of love and acceptance.

I Wanted to Give Up

I never truly realized the power of human touch until the summer after my senior year of high school. My youth group had decided to take a mission trip in the States and work on an Indian reservation for a few days. Before we got there, we were told a little about the culture and the kids. The reservation was nearly 100 percent alcoholic. The abuse rate was almost that high. And the kids would steal almost anything in your possession in order for you to chase them so they could feel someone's embrace.

But my sheltered mind couldn't really comprehend any of this until I arrived and experienced it for myself. And did I ever experience it! I had never wanted to give up on anything in my entire life as much as I wanted to give up on those kids after that first day. They were so violent and abusive to each other and to the sponsors that I just couldn't understand how any of them could react positively to any human touch. But our devotion time that night (without the kids) was so powerful that I actually gave them a shot the next day and let God use me.

My Eyes Were Opened

My eyes have never been opened any clearer than they were that week. Unexplainable as it may be, I will never forget the looks in the eyes of those kids when we embraced them and they knew we were there because of love—love for them and love for our master.

I learned a very important lesson. Although we do not encounter lepers every day, and Jesus is not standing there to heal them, there are still people who need the touch of acceptance. And we can be there to touch them for Jesus.

A quote by Steve Sjogren in his book *Conspiracy of Kindness* sums up what I learned: "It seems that people don't necessarily remember what they are told of God's love, but they never forget what they have experienced of God's love. We cannot love people without first accepting them. . . . An experience of love opens a person's heart to a message of love."[1]

---

[1] Steve Sjogren, *Conspiracy of Kindness: A Refreshing Approach to Sharing the Love of Jesus with Others* (Ventura, Calif.: Regal Books, 1993, 2003), 29.

by Kory Lantz

DAILY WARRIOR

> *I wrongfully believed that you had to be exceptional in order to be influential.*

I'm so glad God uses ordinary people to do extraordinary things—otherwise, I'd be in trouble. I barely made it out of first grade; recess took priority over reading. I love singing, but my voice violates every noise pollution ordinance in the state. I tried dancing . . . once. After unleashing my first move, a friend called an ambulance. He thought I was having a seizure.

For years, I wrongfully believed that you had to be exceptional in order to be influential. Yet Jesus repeatedly changed the world using uneducated fisherman, prostitutes, and disabled people. I bought into God's plan wholeheartedly last summer, and my life hasn't been the same since.

Spiritual Marching Orders

It all started during a mission trip to the Dominican Republic in early summer. There, I felt like my emotions were on steroids. I laughed like I'd never laughed, I cried like I'd never cried, and I served like I'd never served. The smells of poverty and scenes of despair reminded me how desperately our world needs a Savior.

My summer culminated with church camp two weeks before school started. In past years camp promised hours of swimming, laughing with friends, and duct taping a few innocent freshmen to their bunk beds. Yet this year, in my heart, I knew I was on a collision course with Christ.

On the last night my youth leader issued specific challenges for each student. As my turn approached, my knees shook. I knew I would walk away from the evening with my spiritual marching orders for the next year. And sure enough, his first words spoken were, "Kory, God is going to use you in mighty ways this year!" I had no idea how this would play out, but at that point I surrendered all my fears, worries, and future decisions to Jesus.

Blood, Sweat, Mud, and Prayer

Within days of returning from camp, football began and I could not wait to lead the Wawasee Warriors as quarterback for another season. I loved my teammates. Blood, sweat, and mud bond guys together in weird ways. The season opener against an old rival resulted in success, and after the game I felt compelled to kneel in the end zone for a quick prayer. Feeling a little self-conscious, I asked a Christian friend to accompany me. That night, we started the tradition of praying after every game. Each week a few more brave souls would join the group.

After the game I felt compelled to kneel in the end zone for a quick prayer.

After a devastating fourth game loss, I collected my guys for the post-game prayer and headed to the end zone. We started praying, but the approaching noise interrupted us. I could barely believe my eyes. To my surprise, the entire team followed. They slowly took a knee, and I led them in prayer. As I reflect, my prayer actually sounded more like a miniature sermon. I didn't know I had any preacher in me, but the words flowed. In front of my teammates, I thanked the Lord for dying on the cross, forgiving sin, and giving eternal life to those who believed.

Nobody freaked out, and my evangelistic confidence exploded.

Winning Streak and TV Reporters

From that point on our team changed. From a performance perspective, we couldn't be beat. Word quickly spread, and the team vaulted up the state rankings. College recruiters visited frequently, and reporters flooded my high school campus. On the field life was good, but off the field it was even better.

During our hot streak, a statewide television station contacted me. They wanted to do a story on the role faith can play in athletics. For an entire day a reporter followed me to my house, classes, and church. He gave me an opportunity to shoot straight, and I absolutely unloaded the chamber when it came to sharing my faith. Large portions of Indiana watched my story, but most importantly, so did my teammates. Within a few days, three of the most unlikely guys on the team became followers of Jesus after I took them to church.

Given their situations in life, they have an uphill climb, but I am doing all I can to water the seeds that only God can make grow.

Greater Victories

The winning continued, and after fifteen weeks my team earned the privilege to play for a state championship in front of thousands at the RCA Dome in Indianapolis. For forty-eight minutes I lived out a childhood dream. We scored on our first possession, and my teammates joined me in the end zone for what I describe as a very "tasteful" touchdown celebration. They also thanked me for not dancing!

At times I ran for my life from linebackers that I swear were on loan from the NFL. Midway through the game I broke a bone in my passing hand, but the adrenaline kept me going. Sadly, as the final seconds elapsed, I accepted the reality of defeat. It was a hard pill to swallow. Many of us had played together since fourth grade. And now we walked off the field for the final time.

> **My desire to show God's love shifted from obligation to extreme motivation.**

Yet in spite of my on-the-field loss, I could not have felt more victorious. My teammates experienced Christ in a fresh way. A statewide television audience heard a hopeful message. Even my coach commented that I served as his moral conscience throughout the season.

Extreme Motivation

All the athletic success filled endless scrapbook pages, but I knew the experience was only temporary. Finding my life's purpose resulted in the greatest joy. My desire to show God's love shifted from obligation to extreme motivation.

For whatever reason, God's divine plan continually uses normal people to accomplish great feats, and I am a classic example. I'm a normal high school guy. I've never kissed a girl. I used to hold my mom's hand while grocery shopping. It even took me until seventh grade to finally spend the night at a friend's house.

Yet in spite of my fears and weaknesses, God used this daily warrior to change a small corner of the world. I can only believe he wants to do the same with you.

Audience of One

God of the universe
Lifter of my hands
I've failed you many times
But I know you understand
You've given me another chance
And I'm ready to be made new
Come and take this empty life
This time it's all for you

I play for an Audience of One
And my praise has only begun
As the world fades away
I see only your face
And I'm ready to say
I'm yours, here I am

And the world doesn't see
My point of view
But I'm ready to be
A reflection of you
I pray my actions will speak
To the lost and confused
Take me in when I get weak
Let my life be used ... for you

I sing to my Audience of One
And my praise has only begun
As I worship your name
Let the world be the same
Let them find in you true peace
Let this praise never cease
Here I am ... I am yours

by Charity Snavely (written at age 17)

by April Stier

WAITING FOR HARVEST

She sincerely believed her faith was the truth, and I sincerely believed the same about mine.

"Let us not become weary in doing good, for at the proper time we will reap a harvest if we do not give up."

My Bible plopped to the bed. I held my head in my hands as I read Galatians 6:9 again, the words a direct message to my soul.

I wanted to give up. I had been praying for my best friend, a Mormon, for years. The results? Nothing. Nada. Zero. At least as far as I could see. She showed no signs of budging from her faith, and nothing I said or did seemed to make a difference.

A Time to Search

Heather and I became best buds our junior year in high school. Initially, I thought she was a Christian, until we had a conversation at a friend's house one night. We started discussing heaven and hell, and her comments about "outer darkness" and "sons of perdition" caused warning sirens to blare in my mind. I asked more questions about her faith. We engaged in a heavy conversation, both of us insisting our beliefs were correct.

I drove home that night, my faith shaken. She sincerely believed her faith was the truth, and I sincerely believed the same about mine. I knew we both couldn't be right, but how did I *really* know that I was right and she was wrong? I determined to look further into Mormon beliefs.

I bought several books about Mormonism and talked further with Heather. I also sought guidance from my youth minister. My questions caused me to reaffirm the foundation of my faith and the validity of the Bible. I recognized more and more how Mormons have strayed from biblical teachings.

But now what? I felt more solid in my own faith, but I didn't know if I could logically lead Heather out of hers. I'm not a good debater, so I read more books about how to witness to Mormons and took meticulous notes. Then I put my notes into practice.

A Time to Plant

My conversations with Heather didn't go as well as I'd hoped. She had an answer for every argument I produced, and we found ourselves at a standstill once again. Witnessing to her was like trying to climb a wall of Jell-O®—I tried to gain a foothold, only to slide to the bottom again and again.

"Let's just agree to disagree," Heather said. "I don't want to argue about this anymore."

Defeated, I conceded. I felt like a failure, unable to defend my faith convincingly and help her see the problems in hers.

But I couldn't let our differences drop. I knew in my heart Heather was not saved, and I loved her too much to stop sharing the truth. After asking several people to pray for us, I tried witnessing to her again. I really offended her, and she broke off the friendship.

I was devastated. Some Christian friends suggested I restore my friendship with her and ignore our differing religious beliefs. But I couldn't. I'd rather lose a friend by sharing the truth than have an unsaved friend all my life and lose her in eternity.

A Time to Pray

I came close to giving up on Heather during that time. I felt I had done all I could and not made a difference. One morning I cried out to God in pain and frustration.

I'm so bad at trying to show her the flaws in her faith, Jesus. I'm not a quick thinker, and my words get all jumbled. Trying to prove to her that Mormonism is wrong obviously hasn't worked. What else can I do?

The temptation to give up on Heather and move on plagued me. I had done my best. Shouldn't I feel satisfied with that?

I really offended her, and she broke off the friendship.

But I knew I should do more. God clearly had led Heather into my life for a purpose, and he did not remove my burden for her. Heather had cut all contact between us, so I decided to pray regularly for her. Even if we never spoke again, I could still make a difference.

A few months later, God repaired our relationship. I backed off witnessing to her about the false claims of her religion and focused on loving and praying for her. For two years I fasted once a week and prayed for her salvation.

During that time Heather stopped attending her Mormon church. But instead of embracing truth, she walked away from God completely. I battled discouragement many times. God continually reminded me of Galatians 6:9, and I knew that some day Heather *would* be my true sister in Christ if I didn't give up.

A Time to Harvest

That day finally came this year. Her time of living away from God produced some hard consequences. Her life hit rock bottom, and I knew she needed Jesus to help her cope. I shared with her again about God's intense love for her, his grace, and his forgiveness.

Finally one night, she surrendered her life to the Lord. Overwhelming joy flooded my soul. Seven years of prayer, love, and witnessing had finally reaped the eternal salvation of my best friend!

Heather now attends church with me every Sunday. Watching God transform her life has been the greatest blessing—a blessing I could have missed if I hadn't remained faithful. My journey with Heather was anything but easy. But it's all been worth it.

A few days ago, Heather called me from her cell phone.

"What's up?" I asked.

"I was just singing along to a worship song on the radio, and it made me want to tell you something," she said. "Thank you for never giving up on me."

GETTING YOUR HANDS DIRTY

Mission work takes you out of your comfort zone.

Mission trips have been a life and ministry-altering experience for us, the members of ZOEgirl. Each year, the three of us travel overseas with groups to help those who are less fortunate. It's something we plan on doing for a long time.

Strong Reaction

One trip in particular stands out to us. We were in Venezuela. One night we did a concert for the teenage girls who had come on the trip with us. There were almost three hundred girls from all over the U.S. that came. It was right before we were getting ready to record *Life*, our second album.

We played the girls some songs that were possibly going to be on the album. We weren't sure about some of them. Kristin played this song, "Plain," and the response was so overwhelming. We weren't even sure we were going to put "Plain" on the album, but the girls had such a strong reaction that we changed our minds.

After the concert, the girls broke into small groups for some deep spiritual time in which the teens could talk about anything they wanted. Each of us had a discussion with the girls. We said, "Whatever it is in your life that's happening, that's really going wrong, or if you have something you're struggling with, this is your night to be surrounded by support. This is your night to let you know someone understands and is going to be praying for you to help you through it."

The response we received shocked us.

Inspired Ministry

We maybe expected a couple of people to have problems, but we found almost every problem you can think of across the board. Almost every person had something pretty serious that had happened. These were kids from youth groups; I wasn't expecting to hear these issues from so many of them.

You'd think a girl who had raised two thousand dollars to come on a missions trip because she loves God would probably be doing just fine. But there were so many cases of sexual abuse, drugs, alcohol.

We didn't realize it was so prevalent. It really lit our fire to write about those issues more and really reach out to those people.

After the small groups disbanded for the evening, the three of us in ZOEgirl met together. We came back to our room and just sat there with our mouths open, saying, "Wow."

After those conversations, our ministry took on a new meaning. That's when we started realizing how we can use our ministry to address some of those issues. After that trip, we were writing the second album, and we came back with so many new ideas and so much direction from God. That was a pivotal point for us in our ministry.

Changed Perspective

These trips also have inspired us to get as many people as possible involved in mission work. These trips take you out of your comfort zone. Going to another country is a bit scary. You don't speak the language and you don't know the culture. But they're a great way for people to step outside of themselves.

You have to serve on a very gut level, doing whatever you're needed to do.

Mission trips are a great way to get out there and get your hands dirty and not worry about what your hair looks like—just get out there and serve God and see him work in ways you never imagined. They also are a great way to appreciate what you have. Compared to many countries, we are a privileged nation. Granted, there's awful poverty here as well. On average, we have so much more than what other people have in these third world countries. To go to another country and see the needs and what it's like to live without—it's a perspective that more young people in our country should be exposed to so they can understand and really appreciate what they have.

Honestly, aside from knowing Christ, the greatest thing you can do for yourself is go on a mission trip. It will change your life. You can't help but be changed when you go into a situation like that, where you're away from television and music and all the media we're so bombarded with. You have to serve on a very gut level, doing whatever you're needed to do. It will help you find out what you're made of.

Everybody's Calling

Our eyes also were opened to some problems we have living in the United States. As Americans, we're really self-absorbed. Our culture is very focused on self. We need to look beyond that and help other people and not put ourselves first but put the needs of everyone else first, to truly help them and change their lives.

The bottom line for us is that our hearts are focused on missions and serving those around us, whether in America or a third world country. Our calling in life as Christians is to go out and preach the gospel. We might be confined on a tour bus in the United States, but that doesn't mean there aren't other countries that need to hear the good news. People all over the world need to hear about Christ's love and ultimate sacrifice for us. God has taught us so much on these mission trips. It's definitely affected us more than the people we've gone there to affect.

We love being able do something that's really not about ourselves. We love to shovel some dirt for a week or visit an orphanage where no one knows anything about ZOEgirl, and they don't care. It's great to be able to serve on that level.

Ultimately, we believe that's everybody's calling.

by Tanya L. Wells

BEING FRIENDS WITH A WICCAN

At a very difficult time in her life, Tracy felt betrayed and abandoned by the Christian faith.

Warted noses, large black hats, and flying brooms. Those used to be the first images that came to mind when I heard the word *witch*. I never realized how much farther from the truth I could have been.

Religious Differences

In college I was working at an insurance company when it combined with another company. I came in one day to find a new person sitting at the desk across from me.

Right away, Tracy and I hit it off. Both of us were the same age, had a goofy sense of humor, and dyed our hair different colors to fit our moods that month. Not to mention we both liked sunflower seeds for a snack!

But as time wore on, I learned not all was what it seemed. A perfect friendship on the outside was plagued by one major difference—I was a Christian and Tracy practiced Wicca.

When Tracy told me she was a practicing witch, I was taken back. She did not fit the description I always had in my head of a witch. I thought she had to be joking. But she wasn't.

> **I tried to figure out the best way to continue sharing my faith with her and not push her away.**

We often discussed our religious differences. And while we both agreed we would be respectful of each other's opinions, it was hard to not feel attacked at times when Tracy would pose questions to me more in a way to prove me wrong rather than out of curiosity.

Closed Doors

Every day when I arrived home from work, I tried to figure out the best way to continue sharing my faith with her and not push her away.

Over the course of my two-year employment with that company, Tracy and I continued our working friendship, but I never truly felt as though I knew how to reach her or open up the doors of unbiased communication.

You see, Tracy had been raised a Christian. I wasn't talking with someone who knew nothing of God's Word; it was quite the contrary. She seemed to know more than I did. But at a very difficult time in her life, Tracy felt betrayed and abandoned by the Christian faith. How was I to win someone back to the Lord who was convinced he would only let her down—especially when she felt such love and acceptance from the religion she now practiced?

I have to admit that witnessing to Tracy was very difficult for me. And even now, several years later, I look back at the opportunity God presented me and wonder how he judged my feeble attempt to be her friend and a light for his Word.

Fulfilled Duty?

In that situation, I resorted to the tactic of just being Tracy's friend. I didn't point out what I believed was wrong in her life—she already knew what I believed—but prayed she would see the mercy and love of God through my actions and how I lived my life.

After I left that job, Tracy and I lost touch. How were we to keep in contact with nothing in common and no means to force us to communicate?

I often wonder what happened to her and if my little attempt at being a witness to her made any impact on her life. I am not sure I fulfilled the duty God had set before me by allowing us to meet. I can only pray that despite my downfalls as a credible witness for my Lord, what Tracy did see in me as a Christian had some effect on her life.

Despite my questioning how effective I was in talking with Tracy about our differences, God has once again provided me the opportunity to witness to a practicing witch.

And this time it's within my own family.

Another Opportunity

Through the world of Internet conversations and e-mail relationships, I've recently been able to reconnect with a second cousin I haven't seen since childhood. Debbie, like Tracy, is a practicing witch of the Wicca religion. She also is raising her two children to follow the path she has chosen for her life.

Even more than with Tracy, I never would have expected Debbie to take the road in life she has. After all, she was raised in church.

I have talked with Debbie a great deal to learn more about why she chose to follow her "earth religion." She said she found a peace and acceptance she was not able to find in the Christian church and answers to her fears and concerns that no one else seemed able to give her.

> ## *She said she found answers to her fears and concerns that no one else seemed able to give her.*

Debbie also knows what my beliefs are and that because of those beliefs I do not feel her religious choice is correct. But because we love one another as family regardless of our differences, she and I have been able to find a suitable ground on which we can openly communicate our differences and why we believe what we do. Because of that connection, I pray that I will follow God's will for our relationship and that he will use my words and love for my cousin to reach her with the truth of his Word.

"Well Done"

Sometimes, being an in-your-face witness is not always the best approach. We need to get to know the people we have an opportunity to witness to and understand how they will respond to our approaches.

While it is difficult for me to know that someone I love is not right with God, I also believe he has given us free will to choose who will we follow in life. I am not afraid to share my faith with Debbie, although I know she does not share it. But also I must leave the situation in God's hands, praying he will use the times I have to share with her to open her heart just a little bit more to the saving grace of our Father.

I must hope that when I have the blessed opportunity to meet Jesus face-to-face, he will say of my actions: "Well done."

And I hope Tracy and Debbie will meet me there— and hear those same words.

by Christina Dotson

THE ADVENTURE

I had always thought of being saved as a final destination, not a starting point.

Twelve hours after accepting God's gift of salvation and becoming a follower of Jesus, I found myself crammed into the backseat of a van with a half-dozen other teens. My stomach churned and I bit my nails nervously. I felt like I might puke.

What am I doing here? I wondered. *I just became a Christian last night. I'm not ready to share his love with others.*

Yet even as I worried my stomach into knots, Mike's words kept running through my mind. Mike was one of the youth ministers here at the week-long youth retreat I was attending. He was the one who had talked and prayed with me about what it meant to commit myself to the Lord. He was with me through the process of making Jesus my Lord and Savior. I remembered how, afterward, Mike had looked at me and smiled.

"Now the adventure begins," he said.

Before that moment, I had always thought of being saved as a final destination, not a starting point. But according to Mike, the Christian life is an adventure, one in which we continue to grow in Christ every day and help others along the way. That was what we were preparing to do now, and that was what had me scared out of my wits.

Talking to Strangers

The van pulled over to the side of the road, and everyone piled out excitedly. I tried to hang back, but my friend Jamie yanked me out by the arm. "Come on!" she exclaimed. "This'll be fun!"

I could think of many activities that would be more fun than walking up to complete strangers and trying to witness to them—having a root canal, for instance, sounded like a blast right about now—but I didn't say so. Instead I followed Jamie outside to where Mike and the other leaders were unloading three coolers full of soda pop.

The plan was for us to pass out the soda to people in their cars as they stopped at the intersection. Attached to each can was a card with a Bible verse and an explanation that, just like this soda, God's love is free to whoever accepts it.

Quiet and Introverted

Immediately all the outgoing teens—in other words, everyone but me—began loading up on cans of soda. Jamie made her rounds happily, bouncing from car to car like a rubber ball. She chatted cheerfully with every driver, explaining what we were doing and why, and calling out "God bless you!" as each vehicle drove away.

Across the road, two guys from our group were praying with a woman who had pulled off to the side. All around me people were working for the Lord, yet I couldn't bring myself to step off the curb.

"Come on, Chrissy!" Jamie tossed me a can of soda. "What's with you, anyway? You were totally into yesterday's service project."

"Yesterday we were doing yard work for the elderly," I reminded her. "That doesn't involve *talking* to people."

This witnessing to strangers at traffic lights was not my thing.

I had loved the previous day's project. Working up a sweat pulling weeds and trimming bushes was something I was perfectly comfortable with. After all, I had worked as a gardener pretty much since I was old enough to use a shovel. But I was a quiet person. This witnessing to strangers at traffic lights was not my thing.

Please, Someone Else!

As I stood frozen to the curb, I happened to look up the street and notice a small group of city workers filling in potholes. It was a terribly hot and muggy day, and I knew from experience how miserable it is to work outdoors in these conditions. I jogged over to where Mike was still passing out cans of soda.

"Someone should take a few cans to those workers over there," I suggested. "They have to be hot."

"Good idea," said Mike, and he began filling my arms with soda cans.

"Wait a second!" I protested. "I kind of meant someone *else* should do it!"

Mike raised his eyebrows. I felt a need to explain.

"I know I'm supposed to *want* to do this," I sighed. "It's like you're always saying: when we're filled with God's love and grace, we should want to share it others. And I do want to, I really do. I want to grow in

Jesus and share the news of salvation and take part in the adventure of following Christ. I'm just not outgoing enough for this kind of witnessing. I can't do it!"

I fell silent, bit my lip, and waited for my youth leader's response. Yet when it came, it was a surprise.

Nothing on Our Own

"Of course you can't do it!" Mike exclaimed. "You've been trying to get through this by yourself, under your own power. The Christian adventure is not something you embark on alone."

I stared at Mike. He had lost me.

> *"Of course you can't do it! You've been trying to get through this by yourself."*

"Look at it this way," he went on. "You're a gardener, right?" I nodded. "Well, God is like a gardener. Once we accept his gift of salvation, he works in us like a gardener works with plants—watering, fertilizing, pruning. It's God working in us that allows us to grow as Christians. We can't do it on our own. And do you want to know something else?"

"What?"

"Once we let God work in our lives, nothing can stop his work—not setbacks, not other people, not even our own fears." Mike piled two more cans of soda on top of those already balanced in my arms. "So how about it? Do you know what to do?"

I smiled tentatively. I was still scared, but I no longer felt alone.

"Toss another one on top," I said. "There are six workers over there."

God, Work in Me

In the end, I had to call Jamie over to help me carry all the soda. My heart pounded in my chest as I neared the workers at the end of the street.

"Dear God," I prayed silently, "please work in me and help me grow. And give me courage to work for you."

The road workers looked up as Jamie and I approached. I put on my biggest smile and extended a can of cold root beer. "Would you like a soda?" I asked. "It's free—just like God's gift of salvation!"

The workers smiled, accepted the soda . . . and the adventure continued.

FINAL **THOUGHTS**

So now you're finished with this book. You've read many stories of the ways people have encountered God and discovered his sacred calling for their lives.

Now it's your turn.

Don't put this book down and walk away unchanged. Stop for a moment and think about *you*. Have you encountered God's sacred calling for your life? Have you felt his Spirit tugging at your heart? Whose stories in this book do you connect with? What did they say that reminds you of your own relationship with Jesus?

Perhaps you've yet to acknowledge God's plan for your life. Or you might be struggling to see how you can be used for his kingdom. Maybe you've hit rock bottom and wonder why you should even continue on in your relationship with God. Possibly you've turned away from Jesus but are now ready to start over. Or you could be confident in your own calling from God and are now ready to help others recognize God's calling for their lives.

Wherever you are in your relationship with God, he can take you from that point and use you for his glory. It's true! He wants to use you—he made you, he loves you, and he's got great things in store for you. At times, that may be hard to believe. Yet trust that it's true.

So keep listening—he'll be sure to call.

BETHANY DILLON
www.bethanydillon.com

SMALL-TOWN GIRL:

"I come from a big, close-knit family, and we've lived in the same town my whole life," says Bethany, describing her hometown of Bellfontaine, Ohio, which has about 13,000 residents. "It's all so much a part of the music I make, of what I know to be real."

A FOCUS ON FAMILY:

Missions-conscious and service-focused, Bethany's family prays together, plays music together, and loves spending time together. Her parents have been involved in social work for many years, caring for foster kids and adopting two sons. Most importantly, they've instilled in all their children a rich spiritual heritage.

"Even in the moments when I want to give up, when I want to just be careless and act my age and not feel the responsibility that God has given me, I can't help but feel the desire for him," Bethany says. "I can't help but try to follow him. And even that desire is from him. I couldn't do that by myself."

Hear more from Bethany on page 14.

Hector, Melodee, Juan, Megan, Mark, Chris, Andy

CASTING CROWNS

Hector Cervantes—Guitars/Vocals
Juan Devevo—Guitars/Vocals
Melodee Devevo—Violin/Vocals
Megan Garrett—Keys/Vocals
Mark Hall—Lead vocals
Chris Huffman—Bass
Andy Williams—Drums
www.castingcrowns.com

MINISTRY MISSION:

"Sixty percent of my students have probably never heard of the Dove Awards, SoundScan, or radio charts," Mark says about his home church. "These are everyday teenagers living in the real world. Their parents are fighting or their boyfriend or girlfriend just broke up with them and they're failing math. We come home every week to people who desperately need a relationship with Jesus. This is the ministry that God has called us to. . . .

"It's not about art or music. The music is not the point. Music is just a way of sharing the awesome love of God. So we speak of our weakness and our fears—we speak of our failures and how God rescued us from the pit and allows us to be a part of what he is doing in the world. If we are open and honest about our lives and our walk with Jesus, then others will see us and think, 'Hey, that's me too! God can do that in me!'"

FUN FACTS:

Hector's hobby: drawing
Juan's pastime: making videos on computer
Melodee's favorite fun: shopping
Megan's musical amusement: playing bassoon
Mark's not-so-secret joy: playing with his kids
Chris's athletic exercise: basketball
Andy's outside fun: disc golf

Hear more from Mark Hall on page 145.

JEREMY CAMP
www.jeremycamp.com

PERSONAL PAST:

Jeremy met his first wife at a Bible study. The two dated for a bit, but Melissa broke up with Jeremy to spend more time on her relationship with God. After some time, Jeremy found out that Melissa had developed ovarian cancer.

"I walked into the hospital and she was just beaming," Jeremy recalls. "You could tell she wasn't bummed out. She was just trusting the Lord. It was amazing." Melissa told Jeremy that even if she ended up dying from her disease, as long as her death led one person to Christ, it would all be worth it. Jeremy drove from the hospital thinking and praying. "If she tells me she loves me, I'll marry her," Jeremy promised God. It seemed like a fairly safe bet. They had never spoken those words to each while they were dating, why would she say them now?

The words were spoken and the couple got married five months later. But after being married just a few months, Melissa passed away.

PRESENT AND FUTURE:

About two years after Melissa died, Jeremy met his wife, Adrienne, former front woman for the Christian band The Benjamin Gate.

"I knew this pastor who had lost his wife and remarried," Jeremy says. "I asked him, 'How do you love again?' He said, 'Your heart will expand. You're not going to love one more than another. God just expands your heart.'"

Jeremy adds that having children has caused his heart to grow as well.

Hear more from Jeremy on page 184.

UNO Mas, Sharlok Poems, FLYNN, CookBook, Joey the Jerk

LA **SYMPHONY**
CookBook
FLYNN
Sharlok Poems
UNO Mas
Joey the Jerk
www.lasymphony.com

DIFFERENT BUT **UNIQUE:**
"Even though we all do hip-hop, it doesn't mean we like the same things," says CookBook. "We embrace the differences instead of making everyone the same. When we put it all together, it creates a style that none

of us could create on our own. That's what makes the difference. When we come together, it makes for something that's truly unique."

LA HISTORY:

The group came together through mutual friends and by meeting up at the same hip-hop functions. Though each person performed as a solo artist or with another group, the guys started doing their own open mic freestyles and eventually decided to release a project as LA Symphony. Their indie debut in 1999, *Composition No. 1*, quickly landed on the charts and led to an official record deal. In 2001 the group followed up with *Call It What You Want*. They performed at events such as the NBA All-Star Jam Tour. However, on the eve of their proper debut, LA Symphony's label shut its doors and held the group in contract for another two years.

Undeterred, LA Symphony shifted back to the underground by releasing mixtapes, singles, and the hush-hush bootleg *The Baloney EP*. At the same time, the group did shows with the Black Eyed Peas, Xzibit, Good Charlotte, and Public Enemy, among others, in addition to playing the Vans Warped Tour. Finally, with contractual restraints shed, the guys compiled the 2003 disc *The End Is Now*. That album ultimately set the table for the group's 2005 disc, *Disappear Here*, their first commercially released album written and recorded as one cohesive whole.

Hear more from CookBook on page 75.

MAT KEARNEY
www.matkearney.com

HIS STYLE:

Some people have described Mat's sound as Britpop. It's hard to nail down one genre as Mat's voice is compared with Coldplay's lead singer Chris Martin yet Mat incorporates a spoken word style in his songs as well. He even references Johnny Cash in his song "Won't Back Down" from his album *Bullet*. Whatever people want to call his style, Mat is fine. He just hopes people hear the message in his lyrics.

"When I set out to write, I want to write something that will rip your heart out," Mat says. "Hopefully there is a depth and intimacy of the songwriting that goes beyond the novelty of a funky guy with an acoustic guitar. Great songs connect beyond genre and style."

HIS AGENDA:

"My artistic goal was to write something that's 100 percent real and true to me and to this world," Mat says. "I tried to touch on universal truths that really connect with people from every avenue of life. Ultimately, when you write from a vantage point of humility, and you are open to the world around you, people have to respond because those same truths are instilled in them. Honestly, I don't have any agenda other than being sincere, real, and passionate about these songs and the music I make."

Hear more from Mat on page 96.

NICOLE C. MULLEN
www.nicolecmullen.com

LIFELONG DREAM:

From the age of two, Nicole had a mic in her hand, singing with several different family groups in the Cincinnati area. She began writing songs at age twelve, partially as a means of working out some of her own typical feelings of inadequacy as a teenager.

But a high school guidance counselor told her that singers don't usually make enough to earn a living and that Nicole needed to find another line of work as an adult. "OK," she responded, "I guess I want to be a lawyer."

The counselor helped her shadow an attorney for a week. "At the end of the week," Nicole remembers, "the attorney said, 'So, kid, what do you *really* want to be?' I guess he figured I wouldn't be any good as a lawyer. I said I wanted to sing, and he knew I was really passionate about it so he said, 'This is not the life that you really want. Go home and sing.'"

She's been doing so ever since.

BEFORE SHE WAS A STAR:

Nicole began her career in the background, offering support vocals and choreography. Here are some of her credits before the world knew her name:
- backup vocals for Amy Grant
- backup vocals for Michael W. Smith
- backup vocals for the Newsboys
- Dove Award winning songwriter for "On My Knees" that Jaci Velasquez made popular
- voice of the original Larry-Boy song on VeggieTales videos

Hear more from Nicole on page 225.

Ray, Joseph, Jeremy, Joshua

SEVENTH DAY SLUMBER

Joseph Rojas—vocals, guitar
Joshua Schwartz—bass
Jeremy Holderfield—guitar
Ray Fryoux—drums
www.seventhdayslumber.com

FAR FROM FLAWLESS:

"It's always been our goal as a band to really relate to fans, and I think we're able to do that so well because we've been exactly where they are before," Joseph says. "There is so much hurting, so much pain that we see when we look out, and a lot of times living a Christian life can get sugarcoated from the stage. That's just the opposite for us since we'll be the first to share how we've messed up and asked people to pray for us as we're all still far from flawless."

SONG TOPICS:

Some topics Seventh Day Slumber has included in their songs:
- recovery from addiction (written by Joseph)
- being born again (brought firsthand by Ray)
- divorce and rebellion (contributed by Jeremy)
- commitment to sexual purity (conveyed by Joshua)

Hear more from Joseph on page 38.

Chrissy, Alisa, Kristin

ZOEGIRL
Chrissy Conway
Alisa Girard
Kristin Swinford
www.zoegirlonline.com

CHRISSY'S CAREER:

"When I was a teen, I heard about an R&B group that needed a member. I auditioned and made it. The name of the group was Choice, and the members were Sharon, Alecia (the artist now known as Pink), and I. We signed a deal and made an album. After a few years, the label wanted to take Pink solo, and they dropped our group. My world was shattered! Later, I became a Christian. The more I got to know Jesus, the more I realized my life wasn't about what I wanted—but what God wanted to do through me."

ALISA AS A KID:

"As a kid, I had found my purpose in life—gymnastics. But my mom also *made* me take piano lessons (visual: small girl kicking and screaming). I remember hating lessons so much that I dreamed about taking a screwdriver and plucking out all the keys, one by one. When I was eleven, my parents prayed that God would show me his will for my life. Within two weeks, I decided to quit gymnastics and pursue music. It was simple, supernatural, and my heart was filled with a desire for music."

KRISTIN'S CALLING:

"The summer before my senior year of high school, I was attending a convention with my youth group. One evening during a Crystal Lewis concert, I felt the Holy Spirit so strongly. I felt like God was telling me, 'This is why you have such great love and passion for music. I gave this gift to you to use to reach people for me. One day that will be you.' I returned home absolutely on fire, filled with passion, drive, and purpose. That year, I wrote my first song."

More from Alisa, Chrissy, and Kristin on page 250.

TOPICAL INDEX

Interested in a certain topic? Check out the following list and find the stories that relate to you.

ALCOHOLISM 88
Scriptures about getting drunk: Proverbs 23:20, 21; Proverbs 31:4, 5; Galatians 5: 19, 21; Ephesians 5:18

ANGER 188
Results of uncontrolled anger: Genesis 4:1-8
How to prevent anger: James 1:19-21
Expressing righteous anger: Mark 3:1-5; Mark 11:15-17

BIPOLAR DISORDER 150

BREAKING THE LAW 170
Scriptures on respecting authority: Romans 13:3-7; 1 Peter 2:13-17

CONFIDENCE IN GOD 34, 68, 80, 101, 260
Galatians 2:20; 1 Thessalonians 5:24; Hebrews 10:35

CONFLICT 201
How to resolve conflict: Matthew 18:15-20
Conflict-solving in the early church: Acts 6:1-7

DEATH OF A PARENT 75, 206
Isaac and the loss of both his parents: Genesis 23:1, 2; Genesis 24:67; Genesis 25:5, 7-11

DEPRESSION 38, 122
2 Corinthians 1:8-11
Emotions Job felt when hurt: anger, abandoned, and lonely, yet still holding to faith: Job 19:1-29

DRUGS/ADDICTION 38, 214
Romans 6:15-18; Romans 8:5, 6

EVANGELISM/WITNESSING 230, 246, 255, 260
Acts 1:8; Acts 8:26-40; Romans 10:14, 15

FAILURE 68, 135, 155
Gideon felt like a failure, but God used him: Judges 6:11-16; Judges 7
David fails; God gives second chance: 1 Samuel 30

FASTING 72
Instructions on fasting: Matthew 6:16-18
Examples of fasting: Matthew 4:1, 2; Luke 2:36, 37; Acts 13:1-3

FEAR 197
Luke 12:22-31; Philippians 4:6; 1 John 4:18

FORGIVENESS 184, 201
Matthew 18:21-35; Ephesians 4:32

FRIENDSHIP 225, 230, 235, 246, 255
Examples of Christian friends who helped Paul in his ministry: Romans 16:3-16; 2 Timothy 4:9-22
An example of dedicated friendship: 1 Samuel 18:1-4; 1 Samuel 19:1-7; 1 Samuel 20

GENEROSITY 128
Psalm 37:21; Proverbs 11:24, 25; Galatians 6:9, 10
A realization of generosity: 1 Chronicles 29:10-14

GRACE 14, 53, 135
Romans 3:21-26; Romans 4:1-8; Romans 5:12-21

HOMOSEXUALITY 27
Leviticus 20:13; Romans 1:27; 1 Corinthians 6:9, 10
Like all sin, it can be conquered by the blood of Christ: 1 Corinthians 6:11

ILLNESS [PHYSICAL, MENTAL] 131, 139, 150, 159, 194, 206

ISLAM 230
Beliefs to contradict Islam:
We are to follow the example of Jesus, who came to serve, not conquer: Matthew 20:28; John 12:23-26; 1 Peter 2:21-23
We get close to God by developing a relationship with him, not through rituals: Micah 6:6-8; Matthew 12:1, 2, 7, 8; Matthew 15:7-9

JESUS AS A COUNSELOR 63
Isaiah 9:6; Isaiah 11:1-5
Jesus advised his followers—sometimes they took his advice and sometimes they didn't: Mark 10:17-31

JESUS AS A FATHER 175
Jesus showed fatherly love to his followers: Isaiah 9:6, Mark 5:25-34; Mark 10:13-16

JESUS AS A SUPERHERO 19
Jesus' ultimate rescue of us: dying and being raised from the dead for our sins: Isaiah 9:6; Isaiah 53; Acts 2:22-24; Philippians 2:5-11

JOB SEARCH 44
Galatians 6:9

LEADERSHIP 113, 239
Deborah's leadership: Judges 4
Paul's instructions for leadership: 1 Timothy 3:1-13

MENTORING 225, 250
Advice on being a mentor to others: 1 Timothy 4:12
Ruth followed her mother-in-law: Ruth 1–4

MINISTRY [FULL-TIME] 96, 145, 184
Barnabas and Saul called to ministry: Acts 13:2
Paul's charge for Timothy's ministry: 1 Timothy 4:11-16; 2 Timothy 4:1-5

MISSION TRIPS 58, 72, 222, 230, 237, 250
Acts 13–28; also see evangelism/witnessing

MORMONISM 246
Beliefs to contradict Mormonism:
Other religious writings and documents are not equal to the Bible: Deuteronomy 4:1-2; Proverbs 30:6; Revelation 22:18, 19
Other "gods" are not, and could never become, equal to the God of the Bible: 1 Chronicles 17:20; Isaiah 43:10; 1 Corinthians 8:4-6

MUSIC [FINDING GOD IN] 84
Music can communicate core values: Psalm 1:1-3
Music can express anger, frustration: Psalm 137:7-9
Music can tell of the love one has for another person: Song of Songs 4:1-3
Music can tell meaningful stories: Exodus 15:1-10
Music can express the pain, and greatest joys, we feel in this life: Psalm 6:6, 7; Psalm 150:1-6

PARENTS [RELATING TO] 88, 170, 175, 206, 225
Obedience to godly parents provides guidance, safety, a reliable education, stability, and blessings: Proverbs 1:8, 9; Proverbs 6:20-23; Ephesians 6:1-3

PEER PRESSURE 101, 103
Exodus 32:1-6; Proverbs 29:25; Romans 12:2

PRAYER   44, 165, 239
    Matthew 6:5-13; Matthew 7:7-12

QUESTIONING GOD   165, 222
    Job 1:6-22; Job 2:1-10
    God's response to Job: Job 38–41
    Job's response to God: Job 42:1-6

REPENTANCE   170, 179, 184
    Luke 24:45-47; Acts 2:37-39; 2 Corinthians 7:8-11

ROLE MODELS   75, 117
    Older believers as role models: Titus 2:1-8

SELF-CENTEREDNESS   24, 217
    Luke 6:31; Philippians 2:3, 4

SPIRITUAL GROWTH   80, 84, 128, 211
    2 Peter 1:5-11

SUICIDAL THOUGHTS   38, 122
    See Scriptures for depression

WICCA   255
    Beliefs to contradict Wicca:
    God exists apart from nature: Psalm 90:2, 3; Acts 17:24, 25
    Human beings are unique in God's natural creation: Genesis 1:26, 27; Psalm 8:4-8
    Nature has been corrupted by sin: Genesis 3:17, 18; Romans 8:20-22

WISDOM   63
    Psalm 119:33-40; Psalm 119:97-104; Proverbs 2:1-8

True Stories of Teens on a Sacred Journey

ENCOUNTERSWITHGOD

Meeting teens' needs at various places in their spiritual journey—

52 relevant issue-oriented stories and 10 poetic expressions written by teens for teens

Encounters with God, 23354

Order your copy now by calling 1-800-543-1353 or by visiting your local Christian bookstore.

Compiled by Kelly Carr

ref·uge \ ˈre-fyüj \
shelter or protection from danger or distress

"My salvation and my honor come from God alone.
He is my refuge, a rock where no enemy can reach me.
O my people, trust in him at all times.
Pour out your heart to him,
for God is our refuge."
—Psalm 62:7, 8, NLT

In the Old Testament God provided six "cities of refuge" where a person could seek safe haven from vengeance. These cities were places of protection. Today refuge™ will provide you the safe haven you need to grow in your relationship with God.